STUFF THAT MATTERS
FOR SINGLE PARENTS

Stuff That Matters for Single Parents

PATRICIA LORENZ

CHARIS

Servant Publications
Ann Arbor, Michigan

Charis Books is an imprint of Servant Publications.

The following stories were reprinted with permission of *Guideposts Magazine*, Carmel, NY 10512: "Michael's Mouth" (© 1984), "The Adoption of Grandma Sarah" (© 1984), "First Date" (© 1986), "Motorized Mother" (© 1987), "Head of the Household" (© 1989), "On My Own" (© 1991), "The Swill Gang" (© 1992), and "While the Sun Comes Up" (©1992).

Published by Servant Publications
P.O. Box 8617
Ann Arbor, Michigan 48107

Cover design: Eric Walljasper

97 98 99 00 10 9 8 7 6 5 4 3 2

Printed in the United States of America
ISBN 0-89283-955-4

Library of Congress Cataloging-In-Publication Data

Lorenz, Patricia
    Stuff that matters for single parents / Patricia Lorenz.
        p.   cm.
    ISBN 0-89283-955-4
    1. Single parents—United States. 2. Single parents—United States—
Psychology. 3. Single parents—Religious life. I. Title.
HQ759.915.167   1996
306.85'6—dc20   96-11256
                                                      CIP

DEDICATED TO:

Jeanne
Julia
Michael
Andrew

With all my love

Contents

THANK YOU TO:

Ed Kobbeman, my Dad, who inspired my sense of humor, and continues to be a terrific role model and a great friend.

Sharon Hart Addy, whose friendship, writing wisdom, and "get me out of the house!" weekly lunches I treasure.

Alice Zillmer, who told me I was a writer after I wrote my first piece in 1982 and has had faith in me ever since.

All the editors at the magazines and newspapers who have accepted, worked on, and published my articles over the years.

Heidi Hess, my editor at Servant Publications, who helped make the writing of my first book a joyful experience.

INTRODUCTION

~~~

Sometimes I ask myself, "Who am I?"

For years, many women felt they were two things: somebody's wife and somebody's mother. The women's movement gave us a third option: somebody's employee. Superwoman emerged. She not only found time to be all three, she also took classes on the side, exercised regularly, invested successfully in the stock market, and found time to look smashing.

I think that period in "The History of Women" lasted for about three months.

In reality, the blissful, well-to-do, overachieving, "super mom" household with two parents and 2.5 children is rare in today's world. What we have are many, many single parents, both men and women, trying to do a monumental job. And, bless their hearts, they're doing it.

Is it really possible for single parents to do the job alone? No way. That's why this book is divided into three sections: family matters, faith matters, and friendship matters. Quite simply, we need family, faith, and friends to help us.

It's been said that it takes a whole village to raise a child. I believe it. It also takes faith: faith that God will give us generous doses of common sense, so that even during the most stressful times of single parenting we'll somehow end up clearheaded and able to make good decisions for our family. It takes faith that God will protect us and provide us with the answers, even when we're scared to death because we're trying to do a two-person job alone. It takes faith that God will provide when the wolf is precariously near the front door and the savings account is flashing neon red.

Thanks to that beautiful gift of faith and to the emotional support of family and friends, I can honestly say that being somebody's mom has been the most important and the most fulfilling part of my life. God has blessed me with two daughters and two sons, and I've told all of them at one time or another that when I die the most important accomplishment in my life will have been parenting them.

Goodness knows, I didn't always do a bang-up job of it, but I hope that when my last child is an adult, I can say I did the best job I could at the time with whatever reserves of strength, energy, and determination God supplied. Believe me, the good Lord tested me to the limit more than a few times.

Over the years I've heard it all:

"I hate you!"

"Mother, Julia's doing cartwheels in the living room!"

"Mom, is it OK if I invite twenty-five friends over for a party this weekend?"

"Why are you so weird? All my friends get to go to that concert."

"Mom, while you were away at Grandpa's last weekend, Michael had a beer party and the neighbors called the police."

"Why do I need to go to college anyway? Why can't I work in a factory like Tony's dad?"

"Mom, you don't understand me at all. You never listen."

"If I had a dad, things would be different."

"Why can't I have a car? All my friends have cars."

"I'm quitting college and moving to California with my boyfriend."

"Mom, can my band practice in our family room every week?"

"Why can't I ride to school with my friends?"

"I've been arrested for underage drinking."

"Mom, the National Guard called me up for active duty for Desert Storm. I get to skip classes for a week!"

"I know you never wanted to hear this from one of your unmarried daughters, but I'm pregnant."

"Mom, I got sick of messing with my hair so I shaved my head! I love it! Lots of women do it in California! I'm going to keep it this way!"

"I had an emergency C-section last night. It's a girl!"

"Mom, Tim and I are separating."

"Mom, do you think if my dad was alive he would be proud of me?"

"Mom, Tim and I are back together!"

In spite of it all, or maybe because of it all, we five are a family. We love and cherish each other and delight in the times when we can all be together.

I'm no different than anybody else trying to raise kids in today's world. But I do think there's something unique about being a single parent. We single parents get to take *all* the blame for all the mistakes that were made along the way. But then we also get to puff out with pride and joy when our kids turn out OK and we see them raising their children with the same values we have.

What I'm trying to say is that motherhood has been my greatest joy, my most challenging role, and my most cherished accomplishment. Because of it, I've known who I am since 1969, when I became a mother for the first time, and I still know who I am today as I experience the joy of raising my youngest child. Sometimes I think what made it easier is the fact that I like to write. Over the years I've written directives, love notes, and long, long passionate letters to my children. I've written articles about their antics and adventures, and somehow the act of writing about it calmed me down, sorted things out in my mind, and helped me see daylight. And when those articles were published, it also brought me lots of new friends who were going through the same experiences as single parents.

Many of the stories in this book are those articles and letters published over the years in a number of different magazines and newspapers. As I unzip my personal life and open up my heart, it's my hope that your single parenting experience be touched by the grace of God, as mine has been. After all, I've lived to tell about it—and yes, so will you.

PART ONE:

~~~

FAMILY MATTERS

STARTING OVER

꙳꙳꙳

"Pat, I have to tell you something."

"Wait, I have great news! I just talked to the realtor. Our loan was approved. We got the house!"

"Pat, there isn't going to be any house. I just got laid off. We have to leave Denver."

I couldn't speak. Our dream house, the red brick bungalow with the built-in bookcases, a fireplace, and built-in buffet was everything we'd always wanted in a home. My husband and I spent months looking for our first house. Jeanne, our first child, was just a year old. The house was two blocks from a beautiful park with a lake and flower-lined meandering paths, perfect for a mom pushing a stroller.

In spite of my frantic prayers for a quick solution to this disaster, we had to leave our beloved Colorado mountains to start over in Missouri, where my husband had secured a teaching job at a junior college.

Two weeks after arriving in Kirkwood, Missouri, I was surprised to discover that I was expecting another child. While my husband was preoccupied with his new teaching position, I had plenty to do as I unpacked in our new apartment. This one had two huge bedrooms, central air, and even a wonderful swimming pool and play area out back. I rekindled a close friendship with one of my favorite cousins who also lived in the area, and before long, "starting over" didn't seem so bad after all.

In January of 1971 Julia bounced into the world. Seventeen months later, after buying our first home, we welcomed Michael, who was born in May of 1972.

With three children under four years old, our family was complete. But unfortunately, over the next few years, our lives fell apart because of my husband's addiction to alcohol. Extreme unhappiness, frequent abuse, and a sense of fear finally forced me to seek advice from my pastor who agreed divorce was probably the only answer. I pleaded with God to help me change things, but in time the answer was obvious. The children and I had to leave and start over.

On November 13, 1975, after spending most of the day in divorce court, my mother and father helped load the moving truck, and my three children—ages three, four, and six—and I left Missouri, crossed the Mississippi River, and drove up through the state of Illinois to my hometown of Rock Falls.

I'll never forget the first piece of mail I received at our new home, which was actually a ninety-eight-year-old rented frame house. I quickly tore open the envelope.

Nov. 17, 1975

My dearest Patricia.

This little communique hopefully will be the first one arriving at your new home. Welcome home!

For a little while Thursday evening while I was wheeling that big U-Haul eastward over the Mississippi I felt like Moses leading his flock out of bondage.

A great burden has been lifted from our minds now knowing you are free from further abuse. We felt almost helpless to do anything before. Thank God that is all past now.

Lovingly
Dad

That was how my single parenthood began… near the love and support of my parents who were into their thirtieth year of a happy marriage.

Every morning before work my mother stopped in for a visit. The children loved having their grandma around for the first time in their lives. Mom and I drank tea and talked about my job search and about how nicely the house was shaping up with my various rummage sale purchases. The tension that had permeated our lives in Missouri was gone.

"Mom, this old house is wonderful!" I gushed. "The children love their new backyard, the swinging gate, and climbing trees. And the neighbor kids are flocking in from all sides."

The next month I found an interesting job at a radio station and, once again, "starting over" wasn't nearly as scary as I thought it would be. In fact, it was the best time of my life.

A year later when I was broadcasting a parade for the radio station, I met a man who had come from Wisconsin to judge the high school band parade competition. Even though my mother warned me about the seventeen-year difference in our ages, Harold and I continued to see each other every weekend for the next two years.

A few people asked me if I was looking for a father figure. I'd say, "No, I have a perfectly wonderful father. It's just that Harold loves me and the children so much. He's a good father figure for *them*."

When Harold started talking about getting married, I wasn't sure I was ready to "start over" again in another marriage, especially in another state. But Harold was quite persuasive. After a lovely wedding, a "commuter" marriage for nearly three years, and the arrival of baby Andrew, Harold insisted we move to Wisconsin so he could stop his weekend commute.

This time, with four children to uproot and move, a house to sell, a great job to leave behind, and a host of friends and relatives to say goodbye to, it wasn't the easiest "starting over" I'd ever done. But once again, I prayed monumental prayers that it would all work out, turned over all the trust I could muster to God, and in a caravan of cars and a rental truck, the four children and I headed north to Wisconsin.

"Six bedrooms, a big yard, lots of trees? Harold, the house is perfect!" I was thrilled when I saw our new home.

The children thrived in their new school, I found a part-time job at another radio station, the neighbors were exceptionally nice, Harold was happy that he didn't have to commute anymore, and we all loved our new sprawling home.

And so we lived happily ever after, right? Well, not quite. I quickly learned that this older man I'd married did not thrive in a household with three preteens and a baby. The stress of our new blended family (including Harold's six grown children and six grandchildren from his previous marriage) was a bit different compared to the carefree fun and romance we'd enjoyed for the past three years when Harold was still making the weekend trek to our home in Illinois.

The next five years of our marriage was a roller coaster experience. One minute it was Camelot, the next minute unbearable. Before long the unbearable times were the norm. One Sunday afternoon Harold and I sat down and mapped out a plan for an amicable separation that we agreed would only last a year. We both hoped it would give us enough time to figure out how to make the marriage work.

Harold moved to a nice apartment just two miles from our home where he could have some peace and quiet and not be bombarded by the preschool, middle-school, and high-school set. We would visit each other often: date, so to speak. We would also get some serious marriage counseling and hopefully recapture those Camelot days we'd had at the beginning of our marriage.

Two months after we separated, when I thought everything was going great and I was about to suggest making another appointment with a marriage counselor, a stranger came to the door and served me with divorce papers.

"Harold!" I practically hollered into the phone, "We need more time! Why are you doing this?" I was shocked that he wanted to end it completely.

"It's over," he said firmly. "I want a divorce."

Not again. I just couldn't start over again. Not with four children and a two-day-a-week job.

But this time I had fifteen years' worth of "starting overs" under my belt. I'd not only survived each one, but somehow each new start had brought wonderful people and experiences into our lives. *If I just trust in God once again,* I told myself, *I know I can do it.*

The day our divorce was final Harold married a woman closer to his own age who'd never had any children.

Within a month my part-time work at the radio station became a four-day-a-week career. With the help of child support, some extra writing jobs, and the various jobs my teenagers had, we were able to keep going financially and stay in the house we'd all grown to love.

The children and I laughed and cried together, spilt milk without any fog-like tension at the dinner table, created adventures for ourselves, made a home for each other, and figured out ways to get the three oldest through college at the same time.

Harold died of leukemia in 1989, just two years after he remarried. Andrew was nine years old at the time of his father's death. Once again, our lives took on a "starting over" feeling. I wondered if I could raise Andrew alone, without the benefit of his father's love and guidance, but I knew it could be done. After all, I'd learned something many years before in Denver when my dream house evaporated and I had to start over in a new state. I'd learned that "starting over"—after a divorce or in a new job, a new town, a different financial situation; with a new spouse; or after the death of someone you love—"starting over," if you put your trust in the Lord and just bulldoze ahead, almost always means "for the better."

LITTLE RED WAGONS

To be perfectly honest, the first month was blissful. When Jeanne, Julia, Michael, and I moved from Missouri to my hometown in northern Illinois the very day of my divorce from their father, I was just happy to find a place where there was no fighting or abuse .

But after the first month I started missing my old friends and neighbors. I missed our lovely, modern, ranch-style brick home in the suburbs of St. Louis, especially after we'd settled into the old white frame house we'd rented, which was all my "post-divorce" income could afford.

In St. Louis we'd had all the comforts: a washer, dryer, dishwasher, TV, and car. Now we had none of these. After the first month in our new home, it seemed to me that we'd gone from middle-class comfort to poverty-level panic.

The bedrooms upstairs in our ancient house weren't even heated, but somehow the children didn't seem to notice. The linoleum floors, cold on their little feet, simply encouraged them to dress faster in the mornings and to hop into bed quicker in the evenings.

I complained about the cold as the December wind whistled under every window and door in that old frame house. But they giggled about "the funny air places" and simply snuggled under the heavy quilts Aunt Bernadine brought over the day we moved in.

I was frantic without a TV. "What will we do in the evenings without our favorite shows?" I asked. I felt cheated that the children would miss out on all the Christmas specials. But my three little children were more optimistic and much more creative than I. They pulled out their games and begged me to play "Candyland" and "Old Maid" with them.

We cuddled together on the tattered gray sofa the landlord

provided and read picture book after picture book from the public library. At their insistence we played records, sang songs, popped popcorn, created magnificent Tinker-Toy towers, and played hide-and-go-seek in our rambling old house. The children taught me how to have fun without a TV.

One shivering December day, just a week before Christmas, after walking the two miles home from my temporary part-time job at a catalog store, I remembered that the week's laundry had to be done that evening. I was dead tired from lifting and sorting other people's Christmas presents, and somewhat bitter, knowing that I could barely afford any gifts for my own children.

As soon as I picked up the children from the babysitter's, I piled four large laundry baskets full of dirty clothes into their little red wagon, and the four of us headed toward the laundromat three blocks away.

Inside, we had to wait for washing machines and then for people to vacate the folding tables. The sorting, washing, drying, and folding took longer than usual.

Jeanne asked, "Did you bring any raisins or crackers, Mommy?"

"No. We'll have supper as soon as we get home," I snapped.

Michael's nose was pressed against the steamy glass window. "Look Mommy! It's snowing! Big flakes!"

Julia added, "The street's all wet. It's snowing in the air but not on the ground!"

Their excitement only upset me more. If the cold wasn't bad enough, now we had snow and slush to contend with. I hadn't even unpacked the box with their boots and mittens yet.

At last the clean, folded laundry was stacked into the laundry baskets and placed two-baskets deep in the little red wagon. It was pitch dark outside. Six thirty already? No wonder they were hungry! We usually ate at five.

The children and I inched our way into the cold winter evening and slipped along the slushy sidewalk. Our procession of three little people, a crabby mother, and four baskets of fresh laundry in an old red wagon moved slowly as the frigid wind bit our faces.

We crossed the busy four-lane street at the crosswalk. When we reached the curb, the front wagon wheels slipped on the ice and tipped the wagon over on its side, spilling all the laundry into a slushy black puddle.

"Oh no!" I wailed. "Grab the baskets, Jeanne! Julia, hold the wagon! Get back up on the sidewalk, Michael!"

I slammed the dirty, wet clothes back into the baskets.

"I hate this," I screamed. Angry tears spilled out of my eyes.

I hated being poor with no car and no washer or dryer. I hated the weather. I hated being the only parent who claimed responsibility for my three small children. And, without a doubt, I really hated the whole blasted Christmas season.

When we reached home I unlocked the door, threw my purse across the room, and stomped off to my bedroom for a good cry.

I sobbed loudly enough for the children to hear. Selfishly, I wanted them to know how miserable I was. Life couldn't get any worse. The laundry was still dirty, we were all hungry and tired, there was no supper started, and no outlook for a brighter future.

When the tears finally stopped I sat up and stared at a wooden plaque of Jesus hanging on the wall at the foot of my bed. I'd had that plaque since I was a small child and had carried it with me to every house I'd ever lived in. It showed Jesus with his arms outstretched over the earth, obviously solving the problems of the world.

I kept looking at his face, expecting a miracle. I looked and waited and finally said aloud, "God, can't you do something to make my life better?" I desperately wanted an angel on a cloud to come down and rescue me.

But nobody came... except Julia, who peeked in my bedroom door and told me in her tiniest four-year-old voice that she had set the table for supper.

I could hear six-year-old Jeanne in the living room sorting the laundry into two piles, "really dirty, sorta clean, really dirty, sorta clean."

Three-year-old Michael popped into my room and gave me a

picture of the first snow that he had just colored.

And you know what? At that very moment I DID see, not one, but THREE angels before me: three little cherubs... eternally optimistic and once again pulling me from gloom and doom into the world of "things will be better tomorrow, Mommy."

Christmas that year was magical as we surrounded ourselves with a very special kind of love, based on the joy of doing simple things together. One thing's for sure: single parenthood was never again as frightening or as depressing as it was the night the laundry fell out of the little red wagon. Those three Christmas angels have kept my spirits buoyed; over twenty years later, they continue to fill my heart with the presence of God.

THE BAGGY YELLOW SHIRT

~~~

The baggy yellow shirt had long sleeves, four extra-large pockets trimmed in black thread, and snaps up the front... not terribly attractive, but utilitarian without a doubt. I found it in December of 1963 during my freshman year in college, when I was home from school on Christmas break.

Part of the fun of every vacation at home was the chance to go through Mom's hoard of rummage, destined for the less fortunate. She regularly scoured the house for clothes, bedding, and house-wares to give away, then placed the collection in paper bags on the floor of the front hall closet.

Looking through Mom's odd collection one day, I came across the oversized yellow shirt, slightly faded from years of wear, but still in remarkably good shape.

Just the thing to wear over my clothes during art class next semester! I said to myself.

"What? You're not taking that old thing, are you?" Mother chuckled when she saw me packing it. "I wore that when I was pregnant with your brother in 1954."

"It's perfect for art class, Mom, thanks!" I quickly slipped it away in my suitcase before she could object.

The yellow shirt became a part of my college wardrobe. I loved it. It was not only perfect for art class my freshman year, it was also handy and comfortable to throw over my clothes during any messy project clear through my senior year. And even though the underarm seams had to be reinforced before I graduated, somehow I knew there was plenty of wear left in that old garment.

After graduation I moved to Denver and wore the shirt the day I moved into my new apartment. I wore it on Saturday mornings when I cleaned. Those four large pockets on the front, two breast pockets and two at hip level, made a super place to carry dustcloths, wax, and polish.

The next year I married. When I became pregnant with my first child, I found the old yellow shirt tucked in a drawer and wore it during those big-belly days. Though I missed sharing my first pregnancy with my mom and dad and the rest of my family because we were in Colorado and they were in Illinois, that shirt helped remind me of their warmth and protection. I smiled and hugged the shirt close to me when I remembered that Mother had worn it when she was pregnant.

By 1969, after my daughter's birth, the shirt was at least 15 years old. That Christmas I patched one elbow, washed and pressed it, wrapped it in holiday paper, and sent it to Mom. I tucked a note in one of the pockets saying, "I hope this fits. I'm sure the color will look great on you!" I hated to give up the shirt, but I was prompted by something I'd read in Proverbs: "It is possible to give away and become richer!" (Proverbs 11:24). Little did I know how true that would be.

When Mom wrote to thank me for her "real" gifts, she mentioned that the yellow shirt was lovely. Mother never mentioned the shirt again.

The next year my husband, daughter, and I moved from Denver to St. Louis. On the way we stopped at Mom and Dad's house in Illinois to pick up some furniture. Days later, when we uncrated the kitchen table, I noticed something yellow taped to its bottom. The shirt!

And so the pattern was set.

On our next visit home I secretly placed the shirt between the mattress and the box springs of Mom and Dad's bed. I don't know how long it took her to find it, but almost two years passed before I got it back.

This time Mom got even with me. She put it underneath the base of our living room floor lamp, knowing that as a mother of three children all under four, housecleaning and moving lamps were not everyday events for me. "Sneaky" was the only word for that gal!

When I finally found the shirt, I wore it often while refinishing "early marriage" furniture that I found at rummage sales. The walnut stains on the front of the shirt simply added more character to its history.

Unfortunately, our lives were full of stains, too. When my marriage dissolved in 1975 a deep depression overtook me. I wondered if I could make it on my own with three small children to raise. I wondered if I would be able to find a job.

Although I hadn't had much time for Bible reading since my Catholic grade school, high school, and college days, I desperately paged through the Good Book, looking for comforting words. In chapter six of Ephesians, I read, "So use every piece of God's armor to resist the enemy whenever he attacks, and when it is all over, you will be standing up" (Ephesians 6:13).

I tried to picture myself wearing God's armor, but all I saw was me wearing the baggy, stained yellow shirt. Of course! Wasn't my mother's love a piece of God's armor? I smiled and remembered the fun and warm feelings the yellow shirt had brought into my life over the years. My courage was renewed, and somehow the future didn't seem so alarming.

Unpacking in our new home, I knew it was my turn to get the shirt back to Mother. The next time I visited her, I carefully tucked it underneath the winter sweaters in her bottom dresser drawer, knowing sweater weather was months away.

Meanwhile my life moved splendidly. I found an interesting job at a radio station, and the children thrived in their new environment.

A year later during a window-washing energy spurt, I found the crumpled yellow shirt hidden in my rag bag in the back of the cleaning closet. Something new had been added, however. Emblazoned in bright green across the top of the breast pocket were the newly embroidered words, "I BELONG TO PAT."

It took me awhile, but I finally found the solution to the dilemma of how to make it "hers" once again. I gathered my embroidery material. Soon the faded yellow shirt proudly announced, "I BELONG TO PAT'S MOTHER."

Once again, I zigzagged all the frayed seams. Then I asked my friend Harold to help me get it back to Mom.

This was my finest hour. Harold arranged to have a friend of his mail the shirt to Mom from the "Institute for the Destitute, Inc." in Arlington, Virginia. We enclosed a letter on official-looking stationery that Harold had printed in the print shop at the high school where he was assistant principal.

INSTITUTE FOR THE DESTITUTE, INC.

Arlington, Virginia 22204

December 14, 1976
Mrs. Edward Kobbeman
Route 2
Rock Falls, Illinois 61071

Dear Mrs. Kobbeman,

Each year our Institute presents a humanitarian award to an outstanding American for having done unselfish work on behalf of mankind. Your name was submitted to us and placed in nomination along with other individuals and organizations. It is my happy duty to inform you that our Board of Directors has selected you from the list of nominees to be the recipient of this year's award, which is enclosed in the box to which this letter of notification is attached.

Unfortunately, we are unable to make the necessary arrangements for a formal and public presentation. However, we at the Institute expect that the additional and singular honor of being the Bicentennial year winner will provide you with many years of justifiable pride and satisfaction. With our most sincere congratulations, enjoy it in the years to come in multiples of the pleasures we have experienced in awarding it to you.

Admiringly,

Timothy J. Branovan,
President

I would have given anything to see Mom's face when she opened the "award" box and saw that baggy yellow shirt inside displaying my embroidery handiwork. But, of course, she never mentioned it.

On Easter Sunday the following year, however, Mother managed the "coup de grâce." She walked into my home with regal poise, wearing that old yellow shirt over her Easter outfit as if it were an integral part of her wardrobe. I'm sure my mouth hung open, but I said nothing.

During the Easter meal a giant laugh choked my throat. But I was determined not to break the magical unspoken spell the shirt had woven into our lives.

I was sure Mom would take off the shirt and try to hide it somewhere in my home, but when she and Dad left, she walked out the door wearing "I BELONG TO PAT'S MOTHER" like a coat of arms.

A year later, in June 1978, Harold and I were married. The day of our wedding we hid his car in a friend's locked garage to avoid the usual practical jokers. After the wedding, while my husband drove us to our honeymoon suite in Wisconsin, I reached for a pillow so I could rest my head. The pillow felt lumpy. I unzipped the case and discovered a gift, wrapped in wedding paper. I thought perhaps it was a surprise gift from Harold. But he looked as stunned as I. To my complete shock, inside the box was the freshly pressed faded yellow shirt.

Mother knew I'd need that shirt as a reminder that a sense of humor, spiced with love, is one of the most important ingredients for a happy marriage.

Inside one pocket I found a note. "Read John 14:27-29. I love you both. Mother."

That night I paged through a Bible I found in the hotel room and read the verses:

I am leaving you with a gift—peace of mind and heart! And the peace I give isn't fragile like the peace the world gives. So don't be troubled or afraid. Remember what I told you—I am going away, but I will come back to you again. If you really love Me, you will be very happy for Me, for now I can go to the Father, Who is greater than I am. I have told you these things before they happen so that when they do, you will believe in Me.

The shirt was Mother's final gift. She had known for three months before my wedding that she had a terminal disease, amyotrophic lateral sclerosis (Lou Gehrig's disease).

Mother died thirteen months later, at age fifty-seven. I must admit that I was tempted to send the yellow shirt with her to her grave. But I'm glad I didn't, because it is a vivid reminder of the love-filled game she and I played for over sixteen years. Besides, when my oldest daughter started college, majoring in art, I knew that every student needs a baggy yellow shirt with big pockets to wear to art class.

HOW TO SURVIVE MORNINGS

~~~

How does a single parent who works out of the home survive mornings? Easy. Tough love and a few ideas that keep the kids busy and out of each other's hair.

I remember the year my four children were in four different schools. The first school bus arrived at 6:45, the second at 7:10, the third at 7:30, and the last at 8:10.

Instead of turning each morning into a yelling, snapping, "hurry up" catastrophe where Mom has to get up at 5:30 to pull it all off, I decided to make the children 100 percent responsible for themselves.

With the aid of an alarm clock in every room, each child was up between 6:00 and 6:30 A.M. I told the children that if they missed their school bus they'd have to walk to school because I had to go to work and didn't have time to take them. Whoever invented that "tough love" thing is a genius. If walking to school isn't practical, let them call a taxi company and pay for it with their own money. Believe me, it only takes one episode of having a kid walk to school or pay for a taxi ride to cure them forever of alarm-clock abuse.

Another way to avoid early-morning pandemonium is to give them plenty to do. Besides getting themselves ready for school, fixing breakfast, and eating, assign each child one chore to do every morning. Make sure there are dishes to put away from the day before. If you get in the habit of making sure the kids wash and stack the dishes or run the dishwasher the night before, that will provide one child with a great morning chore: emptying the dishwasher or putting away the dishes. That job keeps him or her busy while number two child is setting the table, getting the cereal and milk out, and fixing toast for himself and the one putting away the dishes.

Since two is company and three is a definite crowd in the

kitchen, be sure child number three (if you're lucky enough to have that many) takes music lessons so he or she can spend those early morning minutes practicing. At our house, my eldest hit the piano ivories each morning for thirty minutes.

The next step in the morning survival guide is to tell all your friends and relatives what great kids you have and how every morning they get themselves up, fix their own breakfasts, do their chores, and never miss the bus. If you say this often enough in the presence of the children they'll begin to believe it and instill paramilitary discipline into their own morning routines in order to live up to their reputations.

It helps if the TV is kept off during the mornings lest the little angels get sidetracked by the heart-stopping adventures of old sitcoms and cartoons.

While the kids were doing their thing in the kitchen I'd shower, get dressed, pack my lunch, fix my own breakfast, and organize my day without many interruptions from the children. That's because they were too engrossed to even notice what I was up to. By the time the last bus arrived, I was ready to walk out the door and face the world.

What happens, you might ask, when, heaven forbid, a child tells you that he or she needs a costume or a dozen cookies that day and they forgot to tell you the night or week before? Once again, why panic when, at 7:15 in the morning, you can't possibly do a thing about it?

Simply practice "tough love," teaching your child the consequences of his or her actions. Hug your child and say, "Oh honey, I'm so sorry you forgot to tell me that you needed a shepherd costume this morning. Your teacher will decide if we can work on it tonight or if perhaps someone else will have to be the shepherd."

Somehow I learned early in my career as a single parent that it was imperative to teach my children to be responsible for themselves. Of course, in the mornings I was always there to chat, answer questions, organize the carpooling for the afternoon activities, and kiss them goodbye. But the rest of the morning routine? They did it all, bless their hearts... and we truly did survive mornings.

TWELVE STUPID THINGS

Twelve Perfectly Stupid, Inane, Ridiculous Things
We Parents Constantly Say To Our Children
During Their Growing-up Years

My grandparents said these things to my parents, my parents said them to me, and I've said them to my kids, who will probably say them to their kids. Parents will probably never stop saying these things to their children because 1) parenting is tough enough just trying to get the carpools straight and remembering whose socks have the red rings around the top and whose have the blue, without trying to talk to your children in a way that, goodness gracious, might be somewhat intelligent; and, 2) after giving your life to these creatures who slop peanut butter all over your kitchen, borrow your earrings, and erase things off your favorite computer disk, who has the time to say things that make sense?

Here they are, perfect parent platitudes, time honored, totally meaningless, but, by golly, they get the job done.

1. Because I Said So. This one is first because it's the best. Say it in a voice at least twice as loud as your normal voice with particular emphasis on the SAID part and chances are, four out of ten times, you won't get any backtalk.

2. Watch Your Mouth. Now, really, unless you're standing in front of a mirror, it's physically impossible to WATCH your mouth. But for some unknown reason this phrase can, on the average of 37 percent of the time, get a kid to stop doing one of three things: using bad language, smarting off, or yelling in a disrespectful tone.

3. How Would You Like a…. Depending on the generation and the guilt trip psychologists have dumped on you regarding corporal punishment, this dandy phrase can end with "fat lip," "swat on the behind," "week with no TV, phone, or hairspray," or whatever seems appropriate. Trouble is, someday, somewhere, some kid is going to answer your *"how would you like a . . ."* with "Sure, that'd be great!"

4. Who's the Parent Here, You or Me? Hey, if you haven't figured that out by now, you do indeed have a problem of insurmountable magnitude. A good clue: the parent is the one with dark gray circles under the eyes, caused by excessive worrying or from waiting up until the wee hours for a teenager to return home. The parent may also be the one with zits from eating all the junk food in the house, now that the kid has discovered vegetarianism.

5. Another Think Coming. As in "If you think I'm going to pick up those filthy moist socks and sweat pants and vacuum this pigsty you call a bedroom, you have ANOTHER THINK COMING." Another Think Coming? What, we can only have one think at a time? Uh-oh, here's Another Think Coming, right behind the First Think, and it's crowding the First Think right into oblivion. Give me a break.

6. If Jimmy Played in Traffic Would You Do It Too? You're actually asking your own flesh and blood, who inherited your genes (and probably your jeans), your intelligence, and your personal code of ethics and morals if he or she would actually consider playing in the traffic? Besides, what does playing in the traffic have to do with spraying one's hair with pink and purple glitter paint?

7. Who Do You Think You Are? Well, it's obvious that the tall skinny blond kid standing in front of you is not the black mailman's son, nor is he related to your Chinese neighbors. Actually, he probably knows perfectly well who he is. If *you* have trouble remembering, make a poster of birth certificates and current portrait photos of those who live in your house and hang it in the kitchen.

8. Don't You Think I Know Anything? Believe me, the answer to this question is very obvious, and it's the only answer you're ever going to get. And when you hear it, it's just going to make you mad because all of a sudden you'll start trying to figure out what it is exactly that you *do* know, and when you can't come up with anything, you'll wonder how you got so old so fast. Then you'll just get depressed and, before you know it, you'll even forget what it was the kid said to make you say that in the first place.

9. Over My Dead Body. This tidy phrase does one of two things. A) It puts an immediate end to questions like, "Can I get a mohawk?" "Can I have a boy-girl sleepover?" and "Can I use my savings money to buy a pinball machine?" or B) It gives those little flesh-of-your-flesh mongers thoughts of ways to do you in. Arsenic? Ice cubes on the steps? Bad jokes?

10. Go to Bed, I'm Tired. The logic in this beauty is simply turned around slightly. Go ahead and say it, but wouldn't it be better, actually, to let them stay up until the wee hours while you go to bed? When you get up in the morning, they'll just be dozing off. Before you know it, they'll be thirty-five years old and they might even get an apartment of their own.

11. Because. Never finish this phrase. Treat it like an entire sentence. If you say "BECAUSE I'm tired," or "BECAUSE I can't stand to be around you anymore today," or "BECAUSE your father spent the money on worms," or "BECAUSE Aunt

Gert has taken to the bottle," you're probably giving out too much information. For generations, BECAUSE has been the perfect answer to the question WHY? So don't screw up a good thing. Non-answers like this one also help to keep number four, WHO'S THE PARENT HERE, YOU OR ME? in proper perspective.

12. Someday You'll Understand. The truth here is that no matter WHAT it is you're doing, asking, or saying that needs SOMEDAY YOU'LL UNDERSTAND tagged on at the end, that point in your kids' life when they actually WILL understand is when pigs fly, when Ivory soap sinks, when devils grow wings, when the national debt is erased, or when they have kids of their own.

A DOZEN WAYS TO PARENT WITH LOVE

~~~

Whether you're a young person single-parenting preschoolers, or a middle-ager surviving the zany world of teens, or an eighty-five-year-old grandma who still feels like "mama" to her sixty-year-old son, it's a fact of life: once a parent, always a parent.

Trouble is, we parents will never know for sure what kind of parents we are, especially if we're trying to do the job alone without a lot of help or input from the "other" parent. We'll always wonder if our kids turned out OK because of what we did or because of some other beloved friend, relative, teacher, coach, neighbor, or pastor. And if our kids don't turn out so hot, we'll always wonder if we screwed up or if society failed. We'll always wonder if our being single had anything to do with the kind of job we did, good or bad.

In the meantime, here are a dozen things I learned along the way, after more than a quarter of a century of hands-on, seat-of-the-pants experience.

1. Children Need More Than Things. If you're working extra hours to provide expensive toys, the best label clothes, a library full of video games, fancy cars, or the finest college, forget it. Your children will turn out much better if you forego the "things" and give them your time instead.

If you can't be there when the children get home from school each day, try to arrange for a grandparent (adopt one if you don't have one available) or another relative, friend, or neighbor to be there. And don't think that it's only important to be home with the kids when they're preschoolers. Older kids need loving supervision and someone to talk to after school as much as preschoolers need supervision during the day. Parents and children need to be together as much as possible. Period.

2. Learn from Your Children. When we give birth to a child, we also give birth to two new parents. And we parents have as much to learn about our new role as children do about life in general. Be humble. We have a lot to learn! The best starting point is learning to talk *with* our children, not *at* them. Ask how they feel about certain issues, rules, events. Encourage their conversation. Treasure their input.

3. Forgive Your Children When They Mess Up, and Say "I'm Sorry" When You Blow It. Don't take what they say or do too personally. Once when Andrew, my youngest, was fourteen, he spilled a huge glass of milk on top of the shelf containing my recipe books and into the basket of neatly organized recipe cards. I ranted and raved loudly as I desperately tried to get the milk off every page and every card. When it was over, I apologized. "I know it was an accident. If a friend of mine or a house guest had spilled the milk, I wouldn't have lost my cool at all. So why did I take it out on you?" My wise son answered, "Mom, it's OK. You were just mad at the mess, not at me. You needed to yell, to get the anger out."

Despite what we heard in the movie *Love Story*, it's not true that "love means never having to say you're sorry." If you truly love someone, you're always saying you're sorry! What Andrew said is true. During times of stress, or when our anger buttons are pushed, we often treat those we love the most with the least amount of respect. That's why we parents need to practice forgiveness and teach our children to say "I'm sorry" by saying it to them sincerely every time we lose our cool.

4. Don't Keep Scorecards. When it comes to things your children do that upset you, a short memory is a very helpful thing. "Accentuate the positive, eliminate the negative..." is a great one-liner from an old song, but it's also packed with terrific advice. One way to do that is to buy a large box of those little sticky notes. Every time your child does something positive, write a little love note and stick it where your child will find it.

When Michael, my oldest son, was learning to keep the lid down on the toilet seat, I put a sticky note on the underside of the lid, thanking him for being so considerate. The tiny little love notes I put all over my daughter Julia's room when she was a teenager inspired her to write me long letters that I still cherish.

5. Dirt and Mess Are a Breeding Ground for Well-Being. To expect your child's room to be white-glove-inspection clean at all times is absurd. After all, it's "their" room, not yours, so leave your standards of clean out of it. Teach them how to dust and vacuum and help them organize their closet, desk, and shelf space, then forget it.

Approximately once a year I helped each of my four children reorganize their rooms by getting rid of toys and clothes they'd outgrown, but as far as worrying about the dirt and clutter, I didn't. So far, no one in our family has died from an excess of grime or grossness.

When Jeanne, my oldest daughter, was fifteen and her room was such a disaster of clothes and debris that I couldn't even see the floor, I nagged her for a week to clean it up. One day, in desperation, I dumped everything that was on the floor into a huge black plastic garbage bag and stashed it in a closet in another room. I figured she'd be horrified that half her wardrobe and miscellaneous treasures were missing. Trouble is, she didn't say a word about it for at least two weeks! I don't think she even missed any of it. After that I just kept her door closed so I didn't have to look at the mess. Now, in her mid-twenties, I noticed she was picking up after me when we were on vacation together not long ago.

6. Your Children May Not Be Exactly Who You Think They Are. Why do you think they want a phone in their rooms or the bedroom door closed when their friends are over? As they get older, why do they long to spend more time at their friends' homes or at the mall? It's because they're growing up, getting ready to fly away from your protection to make their own place in the world. They can't be your little darlings forever. They need and want to develop strong personalities of their own. Let them.

Don't think for a moment that everything you think about your children is necessarily true. At some point in their teenage years, they will probably be more willing to share their most personal thoughts and dreams with a total stranger than with you. And that's OK. It's part of breaking away. After all, our job as parents is to help them fray those apron strings. Sometimes it takes a lot of friction to do the job.

Simply put, it's our duty as parents to teach our little birds how to fly away from us. Sometimes we even have to gently push them off that home branch so they can fly away on their own.

7. Stay out of Their Rooms after Puberty. Just make sure they return old food to the kitchen and bring smelly socks and sweaty t-shirts to the laundry room once a week, but other than that, every teenager needs an island to call his or her own. If possible, fix up a good reading lamp and a comfortable chair in there. Make sure there's a desk for homework and a full-length mirror for checking, every twenty minutes or so, to see if the mustache is coming in yet or if that upper arm pec is any bigger tonight than last night.

Even if your teen just sits there listening to awful music and staring into space, he or she needs a place to be alone to sort out the mumble-jumble of thoughts and feelings that carry them through the journey toward adulthood. Privacy is very important as they get closer to the "real" world. They need time and a private place to write notes to their friends, draw cartoons, write poetry, or just daydream.

8. Be Nice to Your Children's Friends. Make them feel welcome in your home. Invite them over for dinner. Fix them after-school snacks. Take them to a ball game or movie with your family. The better you know your children's friends and the more time you spend with them, the more comfortable they'll be around you. If they know that your home is one where they can congregate to gab, eat, play games, and just "hang out," chances are you won't be worrying and wondering why your children are always asking to go to so-and-so's house. It's better to keep the gang at your house by being friendly and respectful of their needs. Convert the basement or rec room into a playroom or teen room. You can always redecorate later when they're out on their own. But for now, home is the best place they can be.

9. Stay out of Their Friendships and Love Lives unless Invited in. Once when Andrew told me his best friend's girl broke up with him, I mentioned it the next time I saw the friend. "Sorry to hear about your girlfriend, Bill," I said sympathetically when it was my turn to drive for the car pool. Later that night Andrew confronted me: "Mom! How could you! You shouldn't have said anything to Bill. Now he won't tell me anything!" I learned a good lesson. Keep the conversation with your children's friends to sports, school activities, and the movies. Kids need to have a life that we're not a part of. That sense of autonomy is as necessary for a growing teen as fertilizer is for a healthy crop.

If, on the other hand, your child chooses friends who are definitely big trouble, into drugs, drinking, or other abusive behavior, we parents need to step in. Just because we're single parents doesn't mean we can overlook obvious problems with our children's friends. Try talking to the friend's parents about the behavior. Or take extra time to get to know your child's friend in the hope that you can help eliminate some of the perverse behavior. Sometimes all a wayward kid needs is an adult who will lend a sympathetic ear.

10. Don't Worry if Your Kids Never Seem to Listen to You. Worry, instead, that they are always watching you. The old saying,

"Do as I say, not as I do," spells certain death if you're raising children. If you cheat on your taxes, swear loudly every time something goes wrong, sneak out of the house to have a cigarette, build up outrageous credit card debts, and lie to your friends or relatives, just know that your children will do exactly the same things when they're on their own. The number one commandment for raising children should be "Do as I say *and* as I do."

11. Hug Them Every Day a Dozen Times. It's been proven that babies die without the human touch. I saw an article in the church newsletter once that said we all need seventeen hugs a day. So do it. Hug your teens, tots, and toddlers. Hug them when they leave in the morning and when they return at night. Hug them before bed and "just because" during the day. It's hard to hold a grudge, stay mad, or pout about anything when someone who truly loves you has their arms around you in a giant bear hug.

12. Love Them Forever, but Let Them Go Early. Too many parents talk their children into living at home during their college years and beyond. Are these people crazy? Let the kids go. Living in a college dorm or that first apartment is one of the most valuable parts of growing up. In addition to getting a good education, our children need to learn to be responsible for themselves. That means taking care of their own basic needs of food, clothing, and shelter. If you're still paying their bills, doing laundry, or completing tax forms for your twenty-year-old son or daughter, there's something wrong with the picture.

Remember, the most important role we parents have is to teach our children not to need us. If we've done a good job, they'll love us and cherish us as friends when they grow up. In the meantime our job is to encourage and teach them how to get out into the world and survive on their own.

LETTER TO A
BRAND-NEW TEENAGER

~~~

Sometimes we single parents have so many bottled-up emotions as our children grow and change before our very eyes that we have to search for ways to express how we feel. If we had a spouse at our side to watch with us the miraculous transformation of our children, it would be easy to let those emotions spill out. But as single parents we must find other outlets. For me it was letters. And you know what? I think it's even better if we put our tender feelings down on paper and share them with our children. They need to know how much their lives fill our hearts with awe and love.

Here is a letter I wrote to Julia when she became a teenager.

Dear Julia,

Last summer, when you were twelve, was the most incredible summer of your life. You changed from a temperamental sixth-grader into a lovely, blossoming teenager beginning her journey toward womanhood.

Just think of all that happened to you last summer. You lost three teeth, grew two inches, started your period, started standing up straight, got your hair cut and permed, had your ears pierced, started shaving your legs, lost five pounds, and learned how to dive off the board. All that in three months!

Once in a while I miss the little girl in you. When you were little, I referred to you as my "chunky, blond, dimpled darling" in the letters I wrote to my friends and relatives. You still have the dimples, but your face is thinner now and your smile more assured.

I've noticed lately that I don't even mind going shopping with you anymore. Remember the battles we used to have? You wanted the best brand names because they were "in" at school, and I, being practical and frugal, refused to give in to the label war. But now that you're earning most of your own spending money, it's fun to go shopping with you. I delight in watching you look for bargains and good value in clothes and accessories. (Of course, it's also fun when you talk me into buying one of those giant, warm-from-the-oven chocolate chip cookies that they sell at the mall . . . and then you break it and I get to choose the first piece.)

You are such a good person, Julia. I can tell just by watching you with your little brother. I know four-year-olds can be exasperating at times, but you always manage to come up with the perfect play activity for him. When I'm trying to get supper ready and the kitchen is a flurry of activity and your little brother is driving us all crazy, you're the one who takes him by the hand and reads to him.

I have a feeling you will be a happy person all your life and that you'll be able to handle any situation that comes along. The children you may bring into this world someday will be lucky indeed to have a mother like you.

I like it when you come into my writing room and just sit quietly on the couch, waiting for me to finish typing before you start talking. Then we talk and talk and talk. You're so much more open with me than I was with my mother. She and I really didn't become close friends until after I was married. But you and I seem to be doing just fine in the friendship department.

Certainly I know there are times when you don't like my decisions about what you can do and when and with whom. Or sometimes you complain about the chore list, but that's OK. You'd be too good to be true if you didn't give me a little grief once in awhile! Besides, I know that questioning authority is an important part of any growing-up process.

Julia, I want you to know how proud of you I am. You are a beautiful young lady, in heart and spirit. You are kind, considerate, and caring. Thank you for your love. When you kiss me goodnight, you make me feel like you really want that hug and kiss and that you're not doing it just because it's a habit. Some girls your age don't kiss their parents goodnight. But I'm glad you do and happy you do it with such verve and sincerity. You make me feel loved!

Good luck in junior high school, sweetheart. I know you're going to do just fine. Remember, it's like a job. You work hard and get paid a fair wage. In school you study hard and get good grades. Later on, your education will propel you into the real world with confidence.

Just remember, I will always be your friend and will probably continue to give you advice (even when you don't ask for it) for the rest of my life. In the meantime, I'm enjoying watching you become a woman. Last summer, especially, was a glorious time for me because you changed so much and tried so many new things. You changed from a nervous little caterpillar into a beautiful many-hued butterfly.

This year I'm sure will be just as remarkable. I love having you for a teenager, Julia.

Love, Mom

BATTLES AND BOOTS, PYGMIES AND PYTHONS

Accept the fact: most single parents are poor. It's a simple matter of mathematics.

Take your typical American "Ozzie and Harriet" family with two kids. They're just scraping by, and when Ozzie and Harriet call it quits, things get worse financially because now Ozzie has to find an apartment and pay rent and utilities. Harriet needs a better car to get to work. And now that she's working full-time, she needs a full-time babysitter. And so it goes. A separation or divorce means the available money is now divided between separate households. Everybody involved becomes poorer.

I remember one of those years when I was contemplating divorce. (Single parents usually have a number of years before the fact when we "contemplate" it.) Anyway, I was going over and over the household budget, trying to figure out how I could make my copywriting job at the radio station provide the basic food, clothing, and shelter for four children and me.

It was wintertime and somehow the subject of boots became a hot topic of discussion. My oldest daughter, Jeanne, had just turned thirteen. She was in her first year of junior high.

You remember junior high. That's where all the boys and girls dress exactly alike. The uniform of the day, the week, the year, includes jeans, t-shirts, sweatshirts, jewelry, and gold-filled athletic shoes. They must be gold-filled, or why would they cost so much?

Of course, boots are definitely not part of the junior high wardrobe. But that day in 1982 when my newly emerged teenager and I shopped at fifteen shoe stores for a pair of athletic shoes in just-the-right-style, just-the-right-color, with just-the-right-stitching on the sides and I ended up paying $51.99 for them...

that was the day boots became a part of my thirteen-year-old's wardrobe.

Buying those athletic shoes changed my life. I became the sole caretaker and guardian of those shoes. My voice changed the day Jeanne bopped off the school bus wearing her new part-leather, part-canvas, part-suede, part-rubber, name-brand $52 shoes and promptly walked up the long driveway through five inches of new snow. By the time I stopped yelling at her, my voice had changed from a sweet soprano to something resembling Bette Davis with a cold.

Next came the directive, "If you want to live, you'll wear your boots to school." My thirteen-year-old grunted, groaned, groveled, wailed, wallowed, and whined, but I stood firm. She wore her boots.

A week later our family got out of the car at church and had to either step in or hurdle over a two-and-a-half-foot snowdrift. Next we sloshed and slopped our way to the sidewalk, which was covered with two inches of Milwaukee's gray-black slush the consistency of sno-cones.

I felt snug and secure in my less-than-glamorous black vinyl boots. I turned to usher my daughter into the church pew and noticed she had on her new shoes. No boots.

My eyes bugged out of their sockets. My heart felt like murder was imminent. But my mind was menacingly reminding me that I was in church. I bit a chunk out of my lower lip and with as much control in my voice as I could muster, told her we'd talk about this bootless incident after services.

Church for me that Sunday was not a grace-filled experience. Rather, I spent the time pondering a punishment to fit my daughter's crime. I didn't want to ground her. After three months of winter weather, I'd been looking for ways to get the kids out of the house. Death in the electric chair seemed a bit harsh. Besides, I wasn't sure how to rig one up. So I settled on having her write a two hundred-word essay on "Why I Should Wear My Boots."

What emerged from her room three hours later is more a study of pygmies and pythons than a study of boots. Here it is as only a seventh grader could write it.

"Why I Should Wear My Boots"
by Jeanne Lorenz

According to the Doubleday dictionary a boot is a shoelike covering of leather or rubber for the foot or part of the leg. It also says that a boot is a medieval instrument of torture for crushing the foot and leg.

Boots keep your feet warm and dry. Boots also come in handy if you happened to be walking through the Amazon jungle and this big huge python comes up to you and says, "I think I'll bite your foot off." You'll say, "Not today, buddy. I'm wearing my boots."

And what if, on an expedition through the deep, dark rainforests of Africa, you're attacked by a band of pigmi-cannibals, the kind that only eat the feet. You'll be lucky you have your boots.

I am very thankful I have boots. They keep me company while I'm waiting for the bus. Many people I know aren't as fortunate as I to have boots. Without boots I would have to sit in a desk with wet shoes every day. That is why I should wear my boots. The end.

I reformed. My teenage daughter sometimes wore her boots in snowy or slushy weather after that, but I stopped guarding her new shoes as if I were in charge of the Hope diamond. After reading her essay, I figured her sense of humor was worth at least fifty dollars.

Whenever I got the urge to ask her what those shoe stains were or where she'd been walking in her new shoes, I simply pulled out my favorite essay. "Why I Should Wear My Boots" reminded me not to be so harsh, so loud, or so demanding. Besides, you have to love a kid who spells pygmy with an "i"!

RAISING MICHAEL

◆◆◆

Raising Michael, my third child and first son, was an absolutely joyful experience... until he entered high school. Before that, Michael had been charming, good-natured, helpful, witty, and cooperative. I simply loved being around him.

But something happened during Michael's teenage years. By the time he entered high school, I felt as though I had somehow slowly, and insidiously—become the enemy. I told myself that it was because Michael was hurting over his broken relationship with his father. My ex had gradually distanced himself from our kids ever since the divorce, when Michael was three. This rejection devastated Michael, who lashed out with the full force of his adolescent angst against the only person he must have known would love him anyway—me.

Each day for the next four years Michael made it clear that he didn't like me. He stopped hugging me goodnight. Told me he'd say his bedtime prayers alone. Spent nearly every evening in his room with the door closed. Stopped doing chores unless he was reminded over and over. Complained about having to babysit his little brother without pay, even when I was just running his older sisters to their various activities. When I'd resort to yelling at him out of frustration, he'd clam up completely, sometimes for days at a time.

When I'd suggest a family meeting, he'd say, "We aren't a family, not a *real* family. What we are is a joke."

Michael's jagged words pierced my heart, leaving me feeling frustrated at best and a failure at worst. I'd bite my lip to keep tears from forming, close my eyes, and say to myself, *Of course we're a family! Just minus one adult, that's all.*

I knew how much not having a relationship with his father was hurting my son, but at the time I had no idea how to fix his hurt or his frustration. All I could do was to continue on day after day as his mom, try to be strong, and hope that someday when he was an adult Michael would understand and at least empathize with my role as head of the household.

During those years Michael never got into any big trouble. He was popular at school, made good grades, was into music and sports, and had quite a few friends. But for four years, all through high school, Michael hardly shared anything with me about school, band, sports, friends, or his girlfriend. Whenever I asked him a simple "yes" or "no" question, he made a sound, a two-syllable response that sounded something like "uh-ahm" which was a cross between "uh-uh" ("no") . . . and "mmh-hmm" ("yes"). I must have said, "What did you say?" to that kid at least a thousand times during those years. I was sure he'd grow up thinking his mother was partially deaf.

I'm not proud to admit this, but toward the end of his high school days, the only way I could find out anything about his life was to eavesdrop on his phone conversations outside his bedroom door. Not that you can get much information when you hear just one side of a conversation, but it was better than nothing. At least I heard the names of his friends and a few details about what they were planning to do over the weekend.

I learned during those years with Michael that the most difficult part of being a single parent is saying "no" to your children, providing the same discipline they'd get if they were in a two-parent family. With two parents in the house, when a kid gets mad at one, he usually still speaks civilly to the other. And if both parents stick together in their discipline, the child learns quickly that it doesn't pay to argue the issue.

But when there's only one parent, the arguments can go on for days at a time. Somehow teens think that if they complain long enough and loud enough we'll lose the courage of our convictions and give in just to stop the argument. Sad to say, many single parents do just that.

But for four years I lived by a one-sentence code that pulled me through: "If I just stay strong and do what I think is right, someday Michael will love me and appreciate what I've done for him."

"No, Michael, you can't ride to school with your friends in their cars. The bus picks you up in front of the house. That's how you'll get to school. It's safer."

He grumbled, growled, and groveled. I stood firm and said to myself over and over, "It's OK. Someday, Michael will love me. Someday he'll understand."

"No, Michael, you can't buy a car with your college money. A high school student who's planning to go to college has no business supporting a car. Your earnings must go into your college fund. When you're an adult, you can buy as many cars as you want."

He argued, yelled, and stomped off to his room. I stood firm and repeated my mantra. "Someday Michael will love me and respect the fact that it isn't easy being the single parent of a teenager."

Many times after a particularly bitter argument with my son, I'd write him a long letter to try to help him see the reasoning behind my actions. Here's one of those letters, written in January of his senior year in high school.

Dear Michael:

According to Amy's mother, she had no idea you were planning to spend the night at their house on Saturday after the dance. And when she heard you have five relatives visiting this weekend, she agreed wholeheartedly that the "right" thing for you to do is to be with them all day Sunday. So here's the schedule for this weekend.

At 8 A.M. Saturday you may drive my car to your four-hour test downtown. After the test you may drive to Amy's, spend the afternoon with her, go to the dance (which gets over at 11:00), take her home, and then be home by 12:30.

Sunday morning you'll go to church with your family. Then after our family dinner you may leave to help set up for the concert at the high school.

Sunday night I'll expect you to be here to visit with your relatives who are coming mainly to see and hear the University of Wisconsin marching band that you're planning to get into next year when you go to the university. Since they're leaving early Monday morning and the only time you'll have to spend with them is Sunday, I'm sure you'll agree that this is the "right" thing to do. It's time to put your own wants aside and think of the feelings of others. At least you'll get to spend all Saturday afternoon and evening with Amy.

I don't do things like this to make you mad at me. I already know what you think of me and how you can't wait to get out of the house. I do these things because they are the "right" way to do them. Someday, when you are mature in your thinking about yourself and others, you'll understand. Until then, you'll just have to hang in there and put up with me. I'm not going to compromise what I know is right to avoid being the brunt of your immature temper tantrums, which, by the way, are very typical of adolescents who think they are all grown up, but who have a long way to go. I know you'll get there someday.

In the meantime, I have three other children who love and appreciate me and for now, that'll just have to do. Hopefully, someday you and I can be friends. I know it's not easy to get through these times, but I'm sure you'll manage. I am proud of you and I love you very much, in spite of what you say and do. Please bear in mind that it isn't easy for me these days with the financial strain I'm under. Do you realize that all the working and struggling I'm doing day after day (with no social life whatsoever) is done primarily for my children? I just hope that if you can't appreciate any of it at this time in your life, that you will at least try to coexist with me during the next nineteen weeks as peacefully as you can.

And by the way, next time you make pudding, how about if you save a little dish for me? You see, Michael, "giving" and "consideration of others" is a two-way street.

Love, Mom

All during high school it seemed that all Michael wanted to do was sit in his room or spend time at his friends' houses, especially with his best friend, Tony. Luckily, Tony's parents were friends of mine. I was happy that Michael might pick up a few "guy" traits from Tony's dad, like how to change the oil in the car, fix his own bicycle, make minor repairs around the house, and most of all, learn to respect marriage and moms in particular.

I'm still good friends with Tony's folks, but I have to admit that one of the most heartbreaking days of my life concerned Tony's mother. Michael and I had traveled to a distant high school where he was competing in a music contest. We were walking down a long hallway when he spotted Tony's mom and took off running toward her.

"Hi, Mom!" he said gleefully as they hugged each other in a big embrace.

I thought my aching heart would shrivel up and die right there. Michael had never, ever run up to me with a "Hi, Mom!" and a big hug. Never.

That night I was still feeling the pain of that moment, still feeling jealous over the relationship my son had with his friend's mom. But the more I thought about it, the more I realized how lucky it was for Michael that he chose such a wonderful family to spend time with. Most importantly, with Tony Senior and Carol, Michael would learn firsthand what a good marriage is all about. He'd see a couple relating to each other, laughing together, respecting and loving each other the way married couples are supposed to.

So, the point is, if you're having trouble with your teenager, take heart: The trouble almost never lasts forever. In fact, when Michael went away to college, our relationship slowly moved 180 degrees. As he matured he came to an acceptance that he and his father would probably never be close. And at the same time our relationship, as mother and son, started growing together.

Two months after Michael graduated from college, he married

Amy, his high-school sweetheart. After their wedding Michael wrote me a letter that he tucked in my suitcase when I left on vacation. Part of that letter reads:

Dear Mom,

Thank you very much for everything you've done for Amy and me. Our wedding was better than we could have planned or imagined it could be, and that's mostly because of you! Also our honeymoon was awesome because of your kindness and wisdom. We feel blessed to have such a wonderful Mom.

Love, Michael

Two months after the wedding, Andrew and I went to visit Michael and Amy in their new apartment. Two weeks later I received a note from Michael which, in part, said, "I have so much to tell you that we should just push pause on our lives and spend another long weekend together. Amy and I have decided that we will never let everything take control of our lives. Our 'new' family (they had just learned that Amy was expecting) and our 'old' family will always be *first*. So when are we going to see you next? Love, Michael."

Believe me, if you've got troubles with your teens, just know that in the blink of an eye, they grow up and almost always become your greatest allies. Be strong now. "Tough love" is just that. Tough. But it's worth it in the long run.

These days when I look at Michael I see a strong, mature, compassionate young man who, as fate would have it, is in some ways a lot like his mom, especially when it comes to our faith in God.

My son, the one who couldn't wait to get out of *my* house, is now a high school band director who can't wait for my visits to *his* house. Isn't life funny?

DEAR TOOTH FAIRY

Communicate with my children? "You mean like really talk, face to face, share my feelings, experience closeness based on verbal communication? You've got to be kidding," you may be saying to yourself right now.

More often than not, we single parents find ourselves lost in a sea of too much to do, not enough time to do it, and too many emotional hangups caused or heightened by the very fact that we are "single" parents in the first place.

But there's a way to communicate with our children that's a lot easier and more effective than the constant day-to-day chatter. What is it? Writing.

Ever since the first caveman drew a picture of a chicken on the cave wall to hint to his mate about what he really wanted for dinner, writing has been an effective method of communication. At any rate, it's worked splendidly at the Lorenz household over the years, especially with my daughter Julia. It all started when she was barely six years old.

Dear tooth fairy. Jeanne pulled my tooth out. and it din't blead. But my tooth is there. Love, Julia. Heres my tooth.

Julia's first note was carefully printed in giant letters on three sheets of paper. She taped her tiny baby tooth to the bottom and slipped it under her pillow. Even at age six Julia must have had an inkling that the power of the written word is magical.

Sure enough, along with a shiny quarter, the tooth fairy left her a note about careful brushing and being a good girl and "Whatever you do, Julia, keep smiling. You have a beautiful smile! And keep writing those letters!"

By fourth grade, Julia was learning that handwritten notes could do a lot more than welcome the tooth fairy and encourage Santa to bring her everything her heart desired. One time, after an argument we'd had about why she shouldn't buy a pair of "clog" shoes, she wrote the following:

Mom,
   These are the reasons I want clogs. 1. You've been wanting boots for a long time and finally you get them. Well, I've been wanting clogs for a long time and I have the money now but I can't get them because of you. 2. If they hurt my feet that's my problem. 3. I have shoes that have heels higher. 4. When Grandma gave us the money for Christmas she said we could get whatever we wanted.

Love, Julia

Julia's logical note taught me to tone down my tendency to be a tyrant. Besides, when I read Julia's letter later that night when I wasn't as tired or crabby as when she first approached the subject the minute I got home from work, I was able to take a more careful look at the "clog" issue. After a calm discussion, I agreed that she could spend her Christmas money on the clogs.

She wore them twice and gave them to Goodwill the next fall. But because of her carefully thought-out letter, she learned a valuable lesson—not only about "fad" apparel, but about something even more important. She discovered something about the power of the written word.

As a working mother who often didn't have time for long-winded, no-win arguments with my ever-changing pre-adolescent, I also began to have a greater respect for the written word. Julia and I exchanged notes about boys, homework, phone calls, and her chores at home. Sometimes our notes were simple apologies to one another after we'd had a shouting match.

As she got older, many of Julia's notes and letters to me were just happy thoughts spilling onto paper and left on my pillow to cherish forever. In seventh grade one of her notes, on bright yellow paper decorated with stars and happy faces, proclaimed:

Mom:

Happy New Year!! Michael and I went to bed at ten. Too tired to stay up till midnight. Andrew went to bed at 9:30. Did you have a good time at the party? Whoopee! Again, happy Happy year!!! See you in the morning!!! Ding Dong: Did you think of New Year's resolutions? Ha Ha Ha. Whooooooppeeeeee. Here I come, 1984!

Love, Julia XO

When Julia was in eighth grade, I discovered those wonderful little notes that stick to everything without making a mess. After they left for school and before I left for work, I started writing quick love notes to each of my children and sticking them in their rooms. Julia, not one to ever let a note or letter of any sort go unanswered, responded to my new form of communication at length:

Mom,

Thank you very much for the very thoughtful beautiful note! Those notes make me feel great no matter what kind of mood I'm in! Sometimes they even make me cry because they touch me so deeply! I'm really glad we have the kind of relationship that we do!! Sometimes we have our arguments but I guess that's life with a teenager! Or life with a 39 year old! Ha Ha! I really like watching you get ready for work, because you really look nice and young. And I'm not just saying that. I thought I should tell you that. I love you!

Julia

P.S. It's really hard for me to express my feelings verbally but writing them down is much easier! XOXO

Julia's postscript on that note explained perfectly why the note system worked so beautifully for the two of us. She was going through the normal traumas of adolescence, and I was suffering through some single parenting woes and career problems. For both of us, writing our feelings down on paper was the most effective way to communicate.

Every so often Julia's notes were gentle reminders that things around the house weren't exactly to her liking. And she was learning that the best way to get quick results from me was to put it in writing. This note was written just before she went to an early Saturday morning babysitting job.

Mom, Hi!

Good morning and good-bye! In my room this morning was about five humongous flies! And when I came up to the kitchen there were about ten of them sitting around the sink! Now who wants to eat their breakfast with a bunch of flies!!! Not me! What can we do about them? Gotta go.

Love, Julia

P.S. See ya around dinner time.

I solved the fly problem before high noon that day.

The summer before Julia started high school she left her razor on the tub where her five-year-old brother could have picked it up. I asked what she thought her punishment should be as she stomped off to her room in a huff. An hour later, realizing the seriousness of her mistake, she plopped a beautifully decorated piece of modern art on notebook paper on the kitchen counter. Centered on the paper and outlined in yellow were these words:

> For my punishment I will NOT:
> 1. have a snack after school .
> 2. watch TV in the afternoon.
> 3. go anywhere after school.

Julia never again left her razor on the tub.

Two months later Julia entered a new phase in her life: high school. The first morning we had a fight about eye makeup and whether or not it was appropriate for school. That night I received a six-page handwritten letter from my daughter. Here is the condensed version:

Mom,

I'm sorry if I was acting snotty but it really makes me mad when you don't give me a chance to say what I have to say! When you told me I wasn't allowed to wear eye make-up and told me how ugly it was, you never gave me a chance to say ANYTHING! And you said "I'm not going to argue about it!" Well, if you would "discuss" it with me maybe it would be a little easier for you and me. I think you should be showing me a good example of how both sides can discuss the problem. Maybe instead of telling me how awful my eyes look you could help me fix them. I don't expect to get my way all the time. Maybe you could treat me like a 14-year-old who's experimenting with make-up, trying to get different looks, and not treat me like a 4-year-old who just "plays" with make-up.

Page three of this dissertation from my tormented teen hit me with all the logic she could muster. The amazing thing is that everything she wrote made perfect sense now that I was much more calm and relaxed than I had been the morning of our disagreement.

Julia wrote:

1. I think I'm very responsible and I could learn to put makeup on responsibly in ways that you and I would both like. 2. Why can't you give me a 3-week trial period to test my ability to wear it. 3. You make it seem as though I'm asking so much! I just want a little freedom. 4. You must admit I don't 'cake-on' makeup like some of my friends. I use it conservatively. I read the directions on the package and I read in magazines how to put it on. 5. I'm growing up and I want to add to my looks to bring out my eyes. 6. If you let me wear it I will put it on lighter and make it look better. 7. Last, but not least, I love you! Really I do. And I'm sorry for the way I acted tonight. Julia xoxoxoxo

P.S. I really want to start the school year off with a bang, not a war!

Julia's letter helped me see the issue from a new light and that basically all she really wanted was my help and advice. Her letter also showed that she was willing to compromise, so I gave her permission to wear make-up ever so slightly, which she did, for about a week. After that she decided that putting on eye makeup on school days was too time-consuming and that by the end of the day it left her eyes looking smudgy.

Sometimes, during those years when I had three teenagers and a grade-schooler underfoot—along with all the care and worries of "single parenting" a home as well—my mothering skills became a little frazzled. Worrying about money and my job while at the same time learning how to operate the huge snowblower, keep a fire going in the woodburner, and take care of a rapidly deteriorating automobile caused me to sometimes lose track of my main responsibilities.

As my raw emotions caused my best mothering skills to fall by the wayside, Julia came to the rescue with this note that she placed on my pillow just a few weeks before Christmas:

Mom,

I thought I should send you this little cheer-you-up message. I know what you're going through and I wish I could make all your problems disappear. Unfortunately I can only send you these silly notes and tell you how much I love you. I can't do much about your problems except hope they all go away. You are a great, wonderful, helpful, loving Mom. Don't let the turkeys get you down. SMILE! You are tee-rif-fic!

Love, Julia

There were quite a few times that year when I really uncorked my bottled-up frustration and took it out on the children. I yelled and nit-picked over the dumbest things, often in twenty-minute tirades that left them wilted and me on the verge of tears. After one nasty episode Julia dropped a four-pager in my purse the next morning for me to read at work.

Mom,

I know it's not easy for you and we all understand. Sure, it's real easy to show your emotions but the hard part is being tactful. You've got to learn to forgive and forget. I don't want to sound like your mother because this is only advice from your 15-year-old daughter who loves you very much, but I'm only doing it for your own good (geez, I do sound like your mother!) I think you should go out more and you don't need to bring the whole family when you want some entertainment. Jeanne, Michael, and I are all growing up and have our own interests, ideas, and friends and we need to be able to make our own mistakes and lead our own lives. We'll always be your kids. I think you're afraid you'll lose us and that's not true! Are you still coming to my assembly on Friday? Hope so! I love you! SWAK (sealed with a kiss)

Julia xoxoxo

Just before Julia turned seventeen, I said "no" to her request to attend a New Year's Eve party at a teen club with her friends. I was worried about the holiday drinkers on the roads; my relatives from out of state were visiting us; and Julia had been out a number of times that week already.

Instead of whining or begging in person, Julia retreated to her room to put her feelings on paper.

Dear Mom,

If I stay in one place all night, how can a drunk driver affect me? When I would get back on the road around 12:30 the so-called "drunks" will still be drinking and celebrating the new year, right? Our relatives will still be here Friday, Saturday, and Sunday so I can spend time with them all three days. I've only been out two out of the last eight nights. Plus, I've been babysitting Andrew every day while you work and have done a lot of housecleaning.

After reading her letter, I discussed the party with Julia once again in a calm manner, and I gave her permission to go for a shortened length of time. But when her grandparents, aunts, uncles, and cousins arrived, she decided at the last minute to stay home because our New Year's Eve celebration sounded like more fun. Julia was growing up.

At the end of her junior year in high school, I knew the summer would be chaos with the children at home and me at work, so I posted "Rules and Regulations for the Summer" on the kitchen cabinet. Julia called it the "Death Notice," and her fourteen hundred-word typed response made me feel like I needed to hire a judge to preside over the discussion that followed. Yet after rereading the rules, which were more like "life in army basic training," and after studying Julia's logical reminders of her exemplary past record and her offers to help with her younger brother, I relaxed some of the summer rules. Julia helped me see that trusting my children would bring better results than playing warden. The summer of '88 was one of our happiest ever thanks to another of Julia's "letters to Mom."

In January of '89 Julia turned eighteen. For weeks before her big day, I asked what she'd like to have for her birthday.

"It's nothing you have to buy, Mom. But I'm working on something."

I should have known Julia would be writing me the letter of her life. The Emancipation Proclamation. It started with Webster's definition of an adult. Then she presented the facts.

1. In less than 8 months I will be living on my own. I won't have any curfews. I can talk on the phone when I want and will definitely be making my own decisions.

2. I have acted very grown-up in the past year and feel I have matured by obeying all rules and regulations with very few exceptions.

3. I feel turning 18 and receiving the four things I'm asking of you will help me feel more like an adult.

4. Think back to your 18th birthday and also Jeanne's and I think I deserve this.

5. It costs NOTHING. Just trust... and I do realize if I break this trust I will no longer deserve this.

6. I'm not flying the coop... just taking a walk on the branch of adulthood.
7. On January 4th, 1989 I will legally be able to vote, serve on jury duty, marry without parental consent, get medical treatment without my parents' permission, sue in my own name, sign contracts, and make a will.

And finally, her PROPOSITION:

For my 18th birthday I would like nothing more than to be treated and respected as a grown-up, mature, developed person. I'd like:
1. A later curfew or no curfew at all.
2. Phone calls later than 10 p.m.
3. More freedom to make decisions of my own.
4. To be thought of as a person, as your friend, not just your "youngest daughter."

Now it was my turn. I made notes, then an outline. Julia had certainly taught me the value of thorough preparation when trying to persuade on paper. I sat at my computer rewriting until late at night. I recalled her tooth fairy letters and remembered how we had solved most of her preteen and teenage traumas on paper, logically, quietly, with little yelling or preaching. I remembered how our notes and letters to each other had soothed our jangled nerves and buoyed each other up during the years of the separation and divorce. Now it was time to end Julia's childhood and help her step across that tremulous line into adulthood.

Dearest Julia:
Adulthood isn't a big deal, really. It isn't a sudden jolt of freedom to do what you want, when you want. It's simply being ready to be responsible not only for ourselves but for others as well. It means taking care of "needs" and not just "wants." It's respect for others demonstrated by the way you treat other people on a day-to-day basis. If you truly believe you can think like an adult, then of course I will treat you as an adult.

Then I addressed her birthday "proposition" list.

Concerning the curfew, I simply asked her to be considerate and phone home if she was going to be very late.

As to the phone calls after 10 P.M., I explained that I would never phone my own friends after 10 P.M. It wasn't the considerate "adult" thing to do.

I gladly gave her the freedom to make decisions that affected her (and not me or the rest of the family) and said I would offer my advice or help only if she requested it.

And finally, I ended my long letter to Julia this way:

Yes, of course I think of you as my friend. But I also cherish you as my daughter. From an inexperienced moth living in a protective mother's cocoon, you are now a beautiful adult butterfly, free to explore the world and enjoy the responsibility of adulthood. Julia, I wish you a happy life filled with love and respect. A life filled with good, solid decisions based on good, solid values. I hope you develop the many talents God has given you so you can make the world a better place because you were here. I love you.

Happy birthday, my friend.

Love, Mom

And so, thanks to the many notes and letters we exchanged over the years, Julia and I not only got through the tough times together, but we also learned the value of the written word when it comes to resolving differences and sharing deep feelings for each other.

When Julia left home to start her own life as a full-time college student, I missed her tremendously, but the part of her I treasured most didn't leave at all. That's the part of her nature that insists that all important feelings and emotions be written down carefully and shared with those you love.

Her college letters to me were absolutely wonderful. And since her graduation, her letters radiate the excitement of her own motherhood and her career as a health promotion and wellness coordinator. I just hope that someday soon my granddaughter, Hailey, presents Julia with a letter that starts, "Dear Tooth Fairy."

GREAT EXPECTATIONS
~~~

Deep down, I've always known that I was at least an OK mother. After all, I did read them a dozen storybooks a day from the time they were old enough to crawl into my lap and sit still until they were old enough to start reading to *me*.

I also packed sack lunches and plopped them into the bucket at the bottom of the tree so that, during their mighty tree fort days, they could raise the vittles up by rope and dine in leafy heaven.

I gave my children lots of hugs and did some of those cool things mothers are supposed to do. Except one. I didn't do much academically for them. I didn't encourage them to watch public TV a whole lot. Checking out the new water slide together at a nearby campground seemed like a lot more fun. I didn't take them to the family science lectures at the local university. Growing potato eyes and Sunday school seeds in the kitchen window was enough science for me. I didn't buy the complete set of classics or tell them everything I knew about Shakespeare (which wasn't much) or about Greek mythology (even less).

At some point, when the children were young, the guilt trip started festering. Personally, I think it was all Richard's mother's fault. Richard was this kid a few grades ahead of me in grade school. His mother knew my mother or something like that.

Anyway, Richard's mother tried her hardest to make something of her son. In grammar school when Richard brought home every stray cat, dog, or wounded bird, she decided he would be a veterinarian when he grew up and immediately bought him an entire set of animal encyclopedias.

In junior high, Richard joined the band, mostly because the cute girl who sat in front of him in biology was a star clarinet player. Richard's mother, ooohhing and aaahhhing over "her son, the drummer," decided that he would be a fine musician someday and bought him a complete classical record library plus a sixteen-volume set of "The World's Greatest Musicians."

In high school, Richard wrote a letter to the editor of the newspaper listing five reasons why the boys in his school should be allowed to wear their hair down to their shoulders if they wanted to. Richard's mother, upon seeing the letter, decided that her son would one day be an attorney, a champion of social justice. So for Christmas that year she bought him some preliminary law books.

A few years later, when Richard was struggling with his general studies courses in college, he came upon the scene of a car accident. He quickly folded up his jacket and placed it under the head of a beautiful coed who had fallen off a motorcycle; later, in her apartment, he positioned a bandage over the scratch on her leg. When Richard's mother heard about the accident, she was sure her son would someday become a famous doctor, a surgeon perhaps. That year for Christmas, Richard received—you guessed it—a copy of *Gray's Anatomy* and a subscription to the *New England Journal Of Medicine*.

Well, poor Richard didn't become a vet, a musician, a lawyer, or a doctor. Last I heard he was making his mark as the top used car salesman in a suburb of Chicago. He and the coed from the motorcycle accident are deliriously happy with their five kids, including a set of twins. And Richard's mother? She went into teaching so she could get some use out of Richard's childhood library.

Now let me tell you about *my* mother and the literary influence she had on *my* life. Mother's favorite songs, poems, and classical works that filled my heart as a child weren't quite as intellectual, as scientific, or as socially stupefying as those literary works that Richard's mother provided for her child.

In grade school, during dark winter evenings while we did the supper dishes together, Mother taught me her favorite songs. Things like, "Tangerine, oh Tangerine, ten feet tall. She sleeps in the kitchen with her feet in the hall."

Poetry? Oh, yes, Mother loved poetry. Here's her favorite, the one I asked her to repeat most often:

THOITY DOITY BOIDS
(author unknown)

Thoity doity poiple boids,
sittin' on dee coib oiten' woims,
Choipin' and boipin'.
Along came Hoibie and his goil friend Goitie.
They saw the thoity doity poiple boids
Sittin on dee coib oiten' woims,
Choipin' and boipin',
And were dey pertoibed!

When I was in eighth grade I had to memorize a poem to recite in front of the class. Other kids were doing bits from Shakespeare, Emily Dickinson, and Elizabeth Barrett Browning's *Sonnets from the Portuguese*. Mother suggested this one:

BACKWARDS LAND
(author unknown)

I'd like to live in Backwards Land,
It would be lots of fun.
The moon would shine the whole day long,
At night we'd see the sun.
In winter, it would be so hot,
We'd fan ourselves all day.
In summer, how we'd love to ride
Through snow drifts on a sleigh.
My folks'd say "Don't wash your face,
Don't ever comb your hair.
You haven't had enough ice cream,

You need the biggest share."
Vacation would be nine months long,
And school time only three.
Yes, I'm sure that Backwards Land
Would be the place for me!

I loved that poem, memorized it, and recited it to my peers, amidst great chuckling from the audience. My eighth-grade teacher, Sr. Mary Judith, didn't think it was quite as funny as they did, of course, but at least she didn't ask me to memorize any more poetry.

Well, that's it, a complete wrap-up of my mother's early literary influence on me. Did she fail as a mother in the "educate your children" part of the job description? Have I failed my own children? After all, neither Mother nor I hauled home complete works of English authors or expected our kids to read Dickens and Homer. But Mother did accomplish one thing: with her sense of humor and silly rhymes, she instilled in me a love of the sung, spoken, and printed word.

My own children certainly didn't escape their childhood without liberal doses of "Grandma-type literature." Every night after prayers I sent them off to bed with:

Good night, sleep tight,
Don't let the bed bugs bite.
If they do, get a shoe and
Bop 'em till they're black and blue.

They also learned "Thoity Doity Poiple Boids" and enjoyed the same guffaws and giggles from their friends that I experienced when my mother taught it to me and when I taught it to my children.

At our house when we've finished eating, especially if we've had dinner guests, sometimes the children and I would say, "My gastronomical satiety admonishes me that I have reached that state of deglutition consistent with dietetic integrity." Then we'd see if our guests could figure out what all those big words meant. Of course we loved telling them that all it meant was, "I'm full." But isn't it more fun the other way? Yes, I think my children will be lovers of words after all. It must be genetic.

THE HANDYMAN
~~~

Many single parents, no matter how long they've been "single again," keep going over and over in their minds the big question, "Exactly why did my marriage end?"

After two marriages plus many years of being single, I think I have it figured out. In order to make the marriage machinery run smoothly, one of the partners has to be handy. One of you has to know how to fix things when they go bump in the night. One of you has to have been born with a ratchet wrench in one hand, a power drill in the other, and an innate knowledge of sump pumps, hacksaws, router bits, and engine gaskets.

My first husband was a geologist who knew a lot about rocks and minerals but spent two hours, six beers, and a lot of blue words trying to hang a picture.

My second husband once used a nail the size of a pencil to start the hole in the wall for the bolts that would eventually hold a small medicine cabinet. After he got it "started" with the nail hole, he used the biggest drill bit this side of the Yukon to drill four holes the size of lemons. Then he had to order toggle bolts from Texas to fill up the holes. He created a leverage effect that would have held up Mount Rushmore on that bathroom wall. I discovered this when I tried to rewallpaper the bathroom; when I removed that little cabinet, the whole wall practically caved into the bolt holes.

Anyway, I understand it now. I didn't choose well when it comes to men; neither of them was handy.

And so I've been the sole "head of household" since 1985. A suburban homeowner. At first I was really smug about it all. I figured that since my father is one of those ultra-handy guys who built his own house from scratch in about six months and for the past fifty years has actually fixed every single thing he owns before it broke, I'd no doubt inherited his handyman genes.

All my life I've watched my dad do "handy" things. He built a barn to house his woodworking and auto shop, and included a snazzy apartment upstairs for houseguests. He crafted a 25-person pontoon boat out of a dozen 250-gallon oil drums that he welded together; the topside he created was a '90s version of *The African Queen*. He had restored a herd of antique cars, and kept his own fleet of family vehicles in showroom condition.

Now in his retirement, Dad volunteers for the park district building foot bridges. He creates wonderful wooden gifts for his children. He has welded, sawed, hammered, and repaired himself into the "Handyman's Hall of Fame."

Considering my background, one might think that some of those creative fix-it-build-it handyman's genes might have worked their way into my own personal list of assets, right?

Wrong. I can't even find the spark plugs, let alone change them. I don't have the vaguest idea which wire is male or female, hot or cold.

Oh, I've tried. A few years ago I even learned how to operate the chain saw. The downstairs in my home is heated with a woodburner, and I quickly learned that a pile of woodburner-size wood outside the back door is an absolute necessity. What I had was logs the size of redwoods and a mini-electric chainsaw. Well, I revved up that baby and had so much fun impressing the neighbors with my "Mountain Man" stance that three hours and a pile of cut wood later I decided to trim a few trees. I chain sawed limbs helter skelter. I trimmed off the tiny branches and sawed up the larger ones for more firewood.

Next spring half the trees I'd hacked were dead. How was I to know that there's a certain time of year to trim trees, and that you're supposed to trim branches off flush with the trunk and not a foot out? Are some people born with innate tree-trimming knowledge?

Another time when my "handyman" genes failed was when I decided to take the wallpaper off the bathroom and redo it with another, much more stylish, paper. I ripped the vinyl part off the walls in about three-and-a-half minutes flat. Of course all the brownish papery part I'd so carefully pasted to the walls years earlier remained behind. So I grabbed a sponge and tried to soak it off. As water dripped down my arms and ran off my elbows in rivulets, I grabbed a putty knife and tried to scrape the sloppy mess off the wall. Then I grabbed my hair and started yelling! Finally I grabbed the telephone and called an expert who came out the next day and finished the job for me (including putting up the new paper) for $125. His expertise was probably a bargain, but once again, I felt like a handyman failure.

Then there was the sump pump that kept running and running and running one particularly wet spring. I'd watch the water gush out the little three-foot-long pipe along the side of the house every few minutes. Finally I figured that the same water was just running back down the foundation and into the tank, forcing the sump pump to pump it out again minutes later.

"What can I do to lengthen that three-foot pipe so that the water will drain much farther away from the house?" I wondered out loud. One night during the middle of a rainstorm that was rivaling the forty-day flood, I got desperate. I grabbed my teenage daughter, Julia, drove like a crazed woman on a mission to the nearest hardware store, and bought the first long thing I saw, which happened to be a twelve-foot length of downspout. Julia wasn't too crazy about having to hold the thing to the side of the car all the way home; but she hung on for dear life, and I drove slowly enough to keep the wind resistance from blowing it right out of her hands.

At home in the pouring rain I found a twenty-foot-long piece of black plastic tubing that I jammed into the end of the original three-foot-long drain pipe. I taped it together with about a hundred feet of wide gray duct tape. (What on earth would the less-than-handy people do without duct tape?) Then I slipped that piece of gutter downspout over the somewhat soft black tubing—for support, I rationalized.

The whole contraption looked like a Rube Goldberg invention and was certainly a landscaper's nightmare, but I noticed that the sump pump ran only every hour or so after that. I'm sure a real handyman would have done things much differently, certainly in a way that would be more aesthetically pleasing. But we've established that I'm definitely not a handyman, so you have to give me a little slack.

One year when I took my annual walk around the yard to see what ravages Mother Nature had placed on my home over the winter, I saw to my disgust dozens of bare patches of dirt that used to be grass. A few years before, I'd given up completely on trying to be "handy" with my lawn and paid a company my entire tax refund and half my savings to have the backyard leveled and sodded. It looked like a country club for a year. But what happens to sod that causes those bare spots? I still don't know the answer to that.

At any rate, I figured a few sprinkles of grass seed and I'd be back in the lawn business, right? So I bought a package of grass seed good for twenty-five hundred square feet of lawn. I estimated the bare area to be about two hundred square feet. Naturally I dumped the entire box in that bare patch, knowing the birds would eat most of it. Next, I sprinkled three fifty-pound bags of topsoil over it and set up the hose.

My dad told me later that it didn't take because the bare spots were on a slope and when I watered it all the seed traveled downhill. I do have one heck of a green spot at the bottom of that slope, though.

Then there are the downspouts. None of them are attached to the walls of my house! They just hang there, two stories tall, flapping in the breeze. I don't even know how to begin to solve this one. How does one keep the brackets around one's downspouts attached to an all-brick house? Even the little wooden pegs that the installers drilled into the house to hold the screws have come out!

I have a lot of other questions, too. What's a ratchet wrench anyway? How is it that some people just automatically know which one of those black things in a car's engine is the fuel pump and which is the carburetor? When you're repainting the trim on the house, how much of the old paint do you really have to scrape off? How often are you supposed to have your asphalt driveway sealed?

Why don't I just know these things instinctively, like my dad? Is it a "man" thing? I don't think so. I know women who can shimmy into a Mack truck and change the spark plugs in nothing flat. I know women who can fix a faucet drip and still catch the last half of the "Monday Night Movie." I'm just not one of them.

I think I've finally figured out a way to fix my antihandy dilemma. I'll put an ad in the personals, something like:

Warm, fun-loving, caring, understanding, appreciative, single mother with large house, 2-1/2 car garage, two workbenches, and a pegboard full of tools, seeks handyman to love, honor, cherish, and hold the droplight.

CLOTHES-CLOSET REFLECTIONS

~~~

All mothers of teenage daughters know what it's like. Shopping for clothes with that age group is a test of patience, physical endurance, restraint, and basic human kindness.

"Mother, give it up! These pants are way too baggy!" "They're skin tight!"

"Well, these shoes are OK and they look just like the name-brand ones and they fit OK. But Mother, they don't have that little aardvark on the label, and everybody will know! I'll pay the $20 difference myself for the name-brand ones, OK?"

"When donkeys fly, you will."

"Mom! Do you actually think I'd be caught dead in a dress like that?"

"No, I was thinking more in terms of the homecoming dance, but if you keep talking to me like this...."

Oh Lord, give me patience. Direct me out of this store and over to the place where they sell the warm chocolate chip cookies. Quickly.

After a few dismal, distressing shopping trips with my daughters, trips that practically brutalized me with teenage logic, I decided to let them shop alone from then on with money they EARNED themselves.

Thanks, Lord, for that brilliant idea. Maybe I'll survive single motherhood after all.

Then one day, a few years later, it happened.

"Mom," Julia asked sweetly, "may I borrow your yellow blouse to wear to school tomorrow? And maybe that brown print skirt?"

"Sure, honey!" I practically fell off the stool at the kitchen counter. At last my daughters were growing up. Our taste in clothes was starting to meld. I suddenly felt ten years younger.

A few minutes later, Jeanne passed through the kitchen.

"Mom, could I try on some of your clothes? I might like to borrow your plaid skirt and one of your scarves."

"Help yourself, my dear," I smiled smugly.

Either I'm getting really hip when it comes to clothes, or they've finally discovered sensible fashion, I mused.

Suddenly, single parenthood was fun. Instead of fighting over the cost of clothes and the styles my daughters chose versus those that actually made sense in the real world, visions of new, exciting mother-daughter shopping sprees danced in my head. I saw the three of us lunching together after our shopping adventures, discussing our bargains and look-alike fashions while dining on quiche and croissants.

Right then Jeanne and Julia emerged from my bedroom dressed practically head-to-toe in fashions from my wardrobe, including jewelry and accessories.

"Thanks, Mom! These are great!" they bubbled.

I wasn't so sure about the combinations they'd chosen, but I certainly wasn't about to criticize. After all, I didn't want to ruin this special moment... this tender passage from teendom to adulthood.

"Ya, they're perfect, Mom," Jeanne nodded. "It's nerd day at school tomorrow... you know, everybody dresses up like the fifties, real dorky-like. These things are perfect!"

"Oh..."

Lord, are you there? I need more patience. Lots more. Right this minute, Lord. Are you listening?

YOU'RE *DRIVING* ME CRAZY

❦

"I'm tired of spending my whole life in that car," I scowled as I grabbed the car keys off the kitchen counter. My son Michael had just reminded me that we had to go out to buy his basketball shoes that evening. As a single parent, whenever the four kids needed to be driven somewhere around Oak Creek's sprawling twenty-eight square miles, I was the one who had to do the driving, to the tune of two hundred miles every week.

"Maybe I should have the steering wheel surgically attached to my hands," I quipped the next night. I'd just spent my whole Saturday driving all over Milwaukee County with one or more of the kids in tow.

"Mom, don't forget, you have to take me to the dance at school tonight," Julia reminded, ignoring my lighthearted complaint.

Back home from that jaunt, I collapsed in front of the TV to read the newspaper when suddenly, six-year-old Andrew was at my side. "It's your birthday tomorrow, Mommy, and I don't have a present yet," he whimpered.

Ah, yes, my birthday. I'd just as soon forget, I thought.

"Andrew, last week you said you wanted to buy earrings and that I could help pick them out. That'll be a wonderful present. We'll go shopping one of these days."

"But your birthday's tomorrow! I want to wrap them in the red paper with the hearts and give 'em to you tomorrow!"

How do you say "no" to such a big heart implanted in such a little body?

"All right, Andrew," I sighed. "Let me get my shoes back on. We'll go right now." *More doggone time behind the wheel of that car,* I grumbled to myself.

In the car Andrew entertained me with stories about school,

about how excited he was to be able to spend his savings on my birthday present, and about how surprised his older brother and sisters would be when he gave me my gift in the morning.

As I listened to my youngest child chatter on and on, I realized it was the first time in quite awhile that Andrew and I had been alone in the car.

At the store we browsed through the earring selection, giggling at the strange ones, ooohhing and aaahhhing at the beautiful ones. Andrew pointed to a pair he liked. I reinforced his selection by saying they were not only beautiful, they were also on sale for three dollars, a dollar less than what he had clutched in his cowboy coin purse.

Knowing he'd made up his mind, I said, "Andrew, decide what you want to do while I go over here and buy socks for Michael." I knew he needed to be alone to make the first purchase of his life.

From the next aisle I could hear his pride-filled voice saying, "Yes, please," when the lady asked him if he needed a box for the earrings. "It's my mom's birthday, and I'm going to wrap them in red paper with white hearts."

After a stop for an ice cream cone we headed home. When we arrived, Andrew disappeared into his room with the red paper and a roll of tape.

"Get your pajamas on, honey, then come to my room and we'll read your bedtime story in my bed."

When he jumped in the bed Andrew snuggled close to me. I could tell he was ready to burst with good feelings about the birthday gift.

"Mommy, this is the happiest day of my life!"

"Why is that, honey?"

"It's the first time I've ever been able to do anything for *you*!" Then his arms surrounded me in a spontaneous bear hug. "I love you, Mommy!"

While Andrew plodded out loud through one of his first-grade readers, I thought about my own acts of "giving." I was always *giving* to my children, especially behind the wheel of that car. Yet somehow I was never really happy about it.

Later I tucked this young son with the big heart into his bed. "Goodnight, Andrew. I love you so much. Sleep tight."

"What about prayers, Mom?"

I'd forgotten. "Oh, of course."

I held Andrew's small hands in mine and thanked God for my small son... and for all my children. I asked God to help me be a happier, more cheerful mother.

Later I looked up the verse about God loving a cheerful giver. "Let each one give according as he has determined in his heart, not grudgingly or from compulsion, for God loves a cheerful giver" (2 Corinthians 9:7).

"A cheerful giver." The words stung my conscience. I'd been about as cheerful as a rainy day lately, especially in the car.

I decided at that moment to stop being such a grouch about all the driving. Within days, the children noticed my new attitude. Instead of pouting in the back seat because Mom was complaining so much about having to drive somewhere again, Michael, now fourteen, climbed into the front seat next to me. On the way to band practice or drum lessons, he'd talk about whether or not he should go out for football. He shared feelings about the girl in his class who'd called him the night before, about what he wanted to do with his life, and about whether he should get a job after school.

When fifteen-year-old Julia rode with me, she'd bubble on and on about the latest antics on her cheerleading squad and about the boy who'd asked her to homecoming. She chatted about the student council fund raiser and told me how she'd been getting extra help in geometry from one of her teachers.

On the way to Jeanne's piano lessons, confirmation classes, or play practice, we talked about where she wanted to go to college, what was happening in her art classes, and why she felt her social life was at a standstill.

In the car, the children and I talked and shared, hooted,

howled, laughed, complained, questioned, discussed, and grew closer to each other.

For Andrew, the happiest day of his life had been the day he'd joyfully given something of himself to someone else.

And I learned that, during those busy years when the children were all at home, the happiest times were when I had one of them in the car. A captive audience!

Those moments became an investment in time that I learned to cherish, cheerfully, thanks to a six-year-old boy with a heart as big as a steering wheel!

How to Find Time for You

~~~

Ever wish your days were thirty-six hours long? And that you could sleep for twenty of those hours? Do you describe your single lifestyle as a series of frazzled, dazzled comings and goings? Do you sometimes feel like you're an overloaded circuit about ready to blow? Feel like you're being pulled eight different ways—every way but loose—by your kids, parents, friends, boss, dates, coworkers, and organization members? If you answer "yes" to any of the above, then you need to find some time for YOU.

Besides having careers and children to raise, we single parents of the nineties belong to professional and social organizations, participate in church and school functions, have hobbies, entertain our friends, and find time to exercise. We do it all, but we often don't do it all well because there just isn't enough time!

At one point when I still had four children at home, a counselor helped me face the obvious. I couldn't be it all, do it all, and have it all unless I took time to be myself and to be happy with what I found. But finding time to do that took planning and plenty of determination. Here are four ideas that can help you find time for the most important person in your life: YOU!

1. Superperson Is Out. You say you're somebody's mother or father, somebody's son or daughter, and somebody's employee, but you can't figure out who YOU are? You're probably on *overload*. There's too much jammed into your life and therefore nothing will compute. Learn to accept the fact that you can't be all things to all people all the time.

The first order of business is to give up a few volunteer efforts here and there. Stop saying "yes" to every organization and every friend who asks for your help. Once you become known as the person who takes care of every PTO request, bakes great cakes for every bake sale, writes witty newsletters, volunteers for this committee and that campaign, is willing to drive not only his or her children but the neighbor's as well to every activity from here to there... you're in big trouble. There is an unwritten law that says, "The more you do, the more you're expected to do."

If you find yourself feeling guilty when you say "no" to the barrage of requests, offer positive alternatives instead. Call the neighbors and organize a car pool for those after-school activities your children always seem to be involved in, for example. And don't automatically acquiesce to your children's constant requests to be driven somewhere. There are other ways of getting places: the kids can ride their bikes, they can walk, they can often organize their own rides from a few of their friends' families, or they can plan activities closer to home.

Set a limit for yourself of once a year for helping out at church, school, work, or organizational functions. For instance, you might agree to help with one fund-raising activity, organize one event, help with one telephone campaign, or serve on one committee. When you've completed those volunteer efforts, relax, say "no" to the rest, and enjoy some time to yourself for a change.

At home, urge your children to take a more active role in the care of the house. It may take time, patience, and lots of positive reinforcement if you've already established the you-do-everything pattern, but gradually, with a few gentle suggestions, your "housemates" will begin to see that the care and feeding of the house and its inmates is not your sole responsibility. Sometimes all it takes is a heart-to-heart conversation with your children during which you lay down some ground rules about who's responsible for cooking, dishes, housecleaning, laundry, and yard duty. Divide the work on rotating schedules so that everyone has a chance to move from one dastardly chore to another on a weekly basis. That way no one gets stuck with the same thing, week after week.

2. Stop Feeling Guilty! Even though you want to be just like the mom that married dear old dad, or vice versa, you might discover that activities like making jelly, canning tomatoes, changing your own motor oil, painting the house, sewing your own curtains, or performing a week-long ritual of spring and fall housecleaning, are beyond not only your time limits but your interests as well.

Take stock of your talents instead... all those brilliant things you do at work, home, church, or other organizations. Then go ahead: admit that you've never made a pie crust from scratch, that you only wash the windows in your house once every three years, that you never polish silver, clean gutters, or strip and varnish the woodwork. Stop comparing yourself to your parents' ethic of house, car, and yard work. Your mother or father probably never wrote a computer program, played in a symphony, redecorated a home, sold real estate, traveled extensively, wrote an article, taught reading, created an original oil painting... or whatever it is that you do a little differently or a little better than your role models.

3. Combine Your Interests with Your Responsibilities. Are you resentful that you don't have time to sit down in the evening for an hour to look at the newspaper? Or that the latest magazines always go unread, that you can never find time for the latest bestseller, or that you're so far behind in your correspondence that you'll never catch up? Instead of looking for a large block of time, use the small moments in your life. Pack a canvas bag full of current reading material or letter-writing supplies, and put it in the car or on the stand next to the front door. When you dash out, grab the bag, and while you're waiting—at the dentist's office getting angry because all the magazines are from 1987, or while the children are finishing piano, dance, or tennis lessons, or for the bus or plane or for Mr. Important to show up for your meeting— reach for your "good reading" bag and enjoy, enjoy!

4. Treat Yourself to a Trip. A weekend trip away by yourself every six months or so is the best elixir to ease the overload of your life. A weekend getaway can be as uncomplicated as a hundred-mile drive to visit your folks or as glamorous as a weekend in New York or Las Vegas.

If money is a problem, take on a small part-time job for a month or so. Stuff envelopes for a business, babysit the neighbors' kids, type term papers, or put ten dollars aside every week until you can pay your airfare or gasoline costs. Better yet, include this expense in your yearly budget. Then take off and visit an old high school or college friend or a distant relative. Once you get there, your room and board will be relatively cost-free.

Or if you're feeling really adventurous, go exploring on your own. Once when I visited a small town in northern Minnesota on a writing assignment, I stayed in "Daisy's Motel" for two days by myself and had a marvelous time getting to know the local people, exploring antique shops, and just plain relaxing.

Getting away for two or three days refreshes the spirit. It forces you to relax; puts you in the company of other adults; and is no doubt as good for the friends, family, and coworkers you're leaving behind (they get a break from routine, too). It's also nice for your children to have some time alone with their other parent, or grandparents or a cherished babysitter. It'll be an opportunity for your kids to see that someone besides you can be responsible for their runny noses, ball games, car pools, laundry, notes to the teacher, and doctor's appointments. It's good for them to learn that life goes on even if you leave town for a few days.

Shakespeare said it best: "To thine own self be true." When the time comes for you to lighten that overloaded circuit, do it. You'll like what you find... a happier, relaxed, more fulfilled person. And the nicest part is that your children, friends, family, neighbors, and employers will probably like you a lot better as well.

GO-CART GRANDMA

Even though my grandmother, Emma Schwamberger Kobbeman, died when I was pregnant with my second child in 1970, she was to become one of my all-time favorite role models. The memories I have of her spirited nature helped get me through some rough times during my struggling years as a single parent with four children at home.

Grandma Emma's husband died during the Great Depression, in 1932. She was just forty-two years old and her five children were twenty-three, twenty-one, twenty, nineteen, and twelve. From that day on, she struggled with poverty, single parenting, and trying to find work with a fourth-grade education. She struggled, but she never lost her sense of humor or her spirit of adventure.

Twenty-five years later she was a grandma with two dozen grandchildren. Nearly every year we had a family reunion in the park near her home. Surrounded by her five children, their spouses, and her twenty-four grandchildren, Grandma Emma presided over the festivities.

One of those family reunions remains crystal clear in my memory. It was the time Grandma Emma decided to ride the go-cart. Perhaps she ate too many sweets that day and was on a sugar high, or maybe it was the sight of her entire immediate family gathered together that made her feel especially frivolous. Whatever it was, we held our breath when Grandma made the announcement that she was going for a ride and then, with her hands on her hips and a twinkle in her eye, walked straight over to the go-cart.

The go-cart belonged to her eldest grandson, who had built it from scratch. The body looked rough, but the engine was a piece of mechanical art that Mario Andretti would have been proud of. When Grandma Emma plopped her ample backside down onto the wooden seat and then stepped on the accelerator with her heavy brown oxfords, that little engine threw itself into world cup competition.

Grandma flew across the track and into the baseball field. She would have made a home run except she missed second base by fifty feet. She barely missed the popcorn stand, however, and then headed straight for a forested area that led directly to the river.

Both arms were flailing in panic as she yelled, "Stop this thing! How do I get it to stop?" As she headed for a row of poplars, narrowly missing two oversized oak trees, she must have experienced total body panic. She released both legs from their death-grip on the accelerator and quickly came to an abrupt halt in front of the sacred Indian mounds at the edge of the water in Sinissippi Park. Chief Black Hawk would have been proud of her.

For a woman who grew up on a small farm in Illinois and watched our country change from horse-and-buggy to men-on-the-moon, Grandma adapted remarkably well. The automobile and the airplane, indoor plumbing, industrialization, mass production, frozen foods, space travel, civil rights, and women's rights were all born during her lifetime. From horse-carts to go-carts, Grandma displayed a keen sense of humor, an unbridled spirit of adventure, and a deep faith in God that I will always be glad is part of my heritage.

Somehow, as I walk through this world as a single parent, it's comforting to know that there were other single parents before me who started the adventure years before I did and who survived beautifully with fewer resources than I can imagine. Grandma Emma was one of them.

THE LAST GREAT TEA PARTY

Andrew and I awoke to one of the coldest January days ever recorded in Milwaukee. The actual temperature was twenty-two degrees below zero with a wind chill factor of seventy below. Schools in most communities in southeastern Wisconsin were closed because of the risk of frostbite for children waiting for school buses.

We'd run out of wood for the wood burner during an earlier cold snap, and the furnace was running almost constantly. The house was still cold. I was wearing two pairs of pants, a turtleneck, and a pullover sweater, and was still shivering in the kitchen as I wondered what my son Andrew would do, stuck in the house all day.

Just then my almost-six-foot-tall eighth-grader walked into the kitchen. As I rubbed my arms to ward off a chill, Andrew asked in a perfect British accent, "Say, Mum, don't you think it's 'bout time for a spot of tea?"

I smiled, thinking that there was always something a bit disarming about this boy. But then of course, *all* fourteen-year-olds seem to be a bit disarming, don't they?

In Andrew's case, I've wondered if perhaps part of his unorthodox personality comes from the fact that ever since his father died, he has guarded our mother-son relationship as something unique and precious. Also, I suppose Andrew is Andrew because his ancestors presented him with a bold mixture of both right- and left-brain talents. He enjoys art, music, and theater as much as he does math and science. To me, he's simply an enigma, a cosmic blend. One of those rare people who's both comedian and egghead, politician and therapist.

At any rate, as soon as Andrew, the cocoa drinker, asked about "a spot of tea," I had one of those unexplainable maternal feelings that something magical was about to happen.

As I grabbed the pot to fill it with water, I remembered Andrew's fascination with his Scotch, Irish, English, French, German, and Dutch ancestry and quickly picked up on his English accent.

"Why certainly, my good man. Do you fancy a spot of Earl Grey or jasmine? Irish Breakfast or apricot? What flavor strikes your fancy this brisk morning?"

Andrew's eyes twinkled. He knew the scene was set. From that moment neither of us spoke in our "real" voices.

"Say, Mum," Andrew continued in an amazingly correct English accent, "I've always wondered. What is the difference between 'high' tea and 'low' tea?"

"Well, lad, low tea, often called 'afternoon tea,' is generally served at a 'low' coffee or end table while the guests relax on a sofa or parlor chairs. High tea, you see, is served at a 'high' dining room table in the early evening, our traditional supper hour. More substantial foods are served at 'high' tea."

My British accent was muddled, but I tried hard to mimic the drama in Andrew's more perfected version.

Andrew snapped his hands together. "So, Mum, perhaps we should have 'low' tea on the coffee table in the living room. I'll make the preparations while you put the kettle on."

Before I had time to remind him that I had work to do in my office, Andrew cleared the low, round oak coffee table of magazines and newspapers; grabbed a cotton lace runner off the dining room table; and spread it across the coffee table. Then he retrieved a centerpiece of dried flowers from the chest in the hallway and placed it behind the lace runner.

Just weeks before, on Christmas morning, Andrew had proudly presented me with a small, solid oak mantle clock he'd made in technical education class. Of course, for today's occasion, my most treasured Christmas gift was removed from the fireplace mantle and placed between the centerpiece and the lace runner. The clock's rhythmic ticking, which could now be heard in the kitchen, made it seem that we were actually living in a drafty old English manor outside London.

Next, Andrew opened the doors of the china cupboard in the dining room. He retrieved my small blue and white English tea pot; two delicate hand-painted bone china tea cups and saucers; two champagne glasses; the silver cream and sugar set; and a silver tray.

"I declare, Mum, I can't see my face in the silver. It's in dire need of a good polishing."

"I'll get right on it, Master Andrew," I said with a wink as I turned off the pot of water on the stove. I could tell 'low' tea was going to be a production of some magnitude that would require timely preparation, and there was no sense boiling the water now. Suddenly, the adventure that lay ahead seemed a lot more important than the work I'd planned in my home office.

Andrew set the table with two sandwich plates trimmed with flowers and gold paint that he found behind the silver. Then, in the napkin drawer, he searched for two perfect ones, settling on dark green linen, with a large hand-embroidered yellow leaf on each corner.

After retrieving the silver polish from under the sink, I demonstrated the fine art of silver polishing on the milk and sugar bowls.

"Here, you finish the silver tray while I start making finger sandwiches, my good man."

"Finger sandwiches? You don't mean...!"

As usual, I read his mind before he finished his sentence. It's not a difficult chore once you figure out that most boys his age delight in taking everything you say literally, even if they know exactly what you mean.

"Not sandwiches made out of fingers, you British subject, you, but wee dainty open-faced sandwiches with the crusts cut off that you eat with your fingers. Tiny tidbits, three or four bites each."

I pulled cream cheese and cherry preserves from the

refrigerator. The spice cabinet provided lots of things to mix with the cream cheese... parsley and onion flakes, garlic powder and chives. As I mixed the ingredients and spread it on toasted rounds of french bread I could see a definite look of approval on Andrew's face.

"Here, the silver tray is ready for the finger sandwiches. Gleaming, don't you think?" he proclaimed proudly as a glint of his true English heritage shone through his eyes. I placed the sandwiches, including tiny toast triangles lathered with cherry preserves, on the tray.

"What can we put in these tall fancy dishes, Madam?" my son asked as he dusted the cut-glass champagne glasses that had hardly ever been used.

"A lovely fruit compote, don't you think? Here, slice this banana and I'll cut up an apple. We'll add kiwi, raspberries, and fruit juice. It'll be fit for the Queen Mother herself," I beamed.

As we waited for the water to reheat, Andrew dashed off to his room, where he scoured his collection of one hundred sixty hats, hanging on all four walls, for a proper hat to wear to what was most certainly going to be a very proper "low" tea.

He emerged wearing an all-wool, plaid tam in shades of green, yellow, and white with a snapdown front and a bright yellow pompon of clipped yarn on top. Uncle Bob had purchased it in Scotland years before and donated it to Andrew's hat collection.

Andrew slipped into an old floppy green herringbone sportcoat I'd picked up at Goodwill, and his tall, trim body was transformed into a gentleman as striking as any English Lord.

"Mum, don't you suppose you need a proper hat and skirt for the occasion?"

I headed for my own five-piece hat collection and emerged with a simple beige wide-brimmed straw hat with a single feather protruding off to the side. A long black matronly skirt pulled on over my pants completed my outfit.

We were the perfect lord and lady, about to dine. The tea kettle whistled. As I poured the water into the "proper" pot and added loose Earl Grey tea encased in a large chrome tea ball, Andrew tuned the radio to an FM station playing classical music, then offered his arm as we entered the living room.

As we made ourselves comfortable on the sofa, I wondered if getting ready for our tea party hadn't been more fun than the actual event would be. I remembered, as a child, spending hours building a playhouse out of an enormous refrigerator-size cardboard box. When completed... cut, colored, and decorated... the fun was over.

But I needn't have worried. As Andrew escorted me from the kitchen into the living room where everything was picture-perfect, we began an hour-and-a-half-long visit that was as delightful as it was surprising. For me, it was as if a long-lost relative had popped in for the day.

By now, my character in our "English play acting" had evolved into a sort of beloved great-aunt who doted on her nephew and wanted to know everything about him.

"So, tell me, Sir Andrew, what are your plans? Where are you going in this great adventure of life?"

Andrew leaned back on the throw pillows behind us as he sipped his Earl Grey and stroked his chin. "Well, it's a long road. I still have four years of high school after this year, then college, you know. It's an expensive road, going to college. I wonder, some-times, how I'll ever afford it."

I gently reminded him that financial aid would be available just like it had been for his sisters and brother. We talked about scholarships and how, if he kept his grades up, he might even get into one of his "dream" schools, the Air Force Academy or Notre Dame.

We chatted about girls.

"They all think I'm a geek," he said quietly, without humor. "And I don't know how to fight so they probably think I'm a wuss."

I looked carefully at the tall, lanky young man before me, whose size thirteen feet proclaimed the fact that his six-foot growth spurt wasn't anywhere near over. *Not* fighting was much more manly, I reassured him. And in high school the girls would certainly appreciate his sensitivity and talents.

As the mantle clock ticked on, we talked about music, sports, and the weather. We watched a squirrel on the deck outside the living room windows eating corn off a cob we'd placed outside the day before.

I shared some personal feelings of my own, about how scared I was the year before when I quit my regular job to start a business in my home. I even told this "new and interested" confidant that after six years of being alone I would like to meet someone interesting and perhaps even get married again.

As we sipped cup after cup of tea, we opened up parts of ourselves that neither of us had shared before. We finished the morning by raving about the marvelous finger sandwiches and fruit salad we'd created on a moment's notice. And each time after Andrew refilled my tea cup, he took the tiny tongs and asked, "One lump or two, Mum?"

That cold winter day, when I was forty-eight and Andrew fourteen, I was transported into a world I knew would exist only for that one morning. I knew that when the next day came and school reopened we would never again have a tea party like this one. Andrew would immerse himself in school, the basketball team, music, his friends, the school play, the telephone, and video games at his best friend's house.

But it didn't matter because on that coldest day of the year, during those precious three hours as we stumbled through a mumble-jumble of British phrases and inadequate but charming accents, my youngest child and I ate, drank, talked, shared, laughed, and warmed our souls to the very core.

Andrew and I created a play at the very same instant we performed it. There was no audience. Just Andrew and me, and cups of very good tea.

Roll on, Mama, Roll on!

~~~

When I first heard the words "roller disco," I assumed you had to be under sixteen, into pinball, a rock freak, and have ankles of steel. So naturally, as a middle-aged single parent of four, I avoided the craze like a swarm of bees. But when my three older children begged to go skating at the local roller rink, I figured it would save twenty miles' worth of gas if I just stayed there rather than making two complete round trips. Besides, watching them skate, being there to buoy their spirits and cheer them on, seemed like the noble "quality time" thing to do.

Those kids of mine had their skates laced up and were gliding around the floor before I even found a seat in the snack shop. I soon discovered that sitting around watching other people skate was not a great way to spend an afternoon. Spectator sports have always given me a pain where I sit anyway. So after a few minutes of fidgeting, I gave it the old "what-the-heck" routine, walked over to the cashier, paid my money, laced up my size nine rental skates, and stood up.

Well, now, standing up wasn't so bad. My arms weren't even flailing. Maybe I was a natural. I watched my children gliding around the floor. A heart-throbbing current hit with a heavy beat blared out of the eight oversized loud speakers. It was a song I'd heard on the radio often over the last few weeks, and I sort of liked the rhythm.

I watched the other youngsters move their bodies to the beat of the music. Incredible! They were dancing on roller skates! Every kid in the place was filled with "dance fever." Each one kept time to the music, effortlessly gliding along on eight-wheelers. A tall teenager whizzed by doing gyrations with his legs that Arthur Murray would have applauded.

Now that I had mastered standing up, I wobbled gingerly toward the crowd, feeling more like a preteen trying to get the hang of spike heels than a sophisticated "quality time seeker" single mom.

I noticed everyone was skating in a big oval, round and round in the same direction. I chose a spot where the crowd seemed a bit thinner and darted.... no, make that shimmied, onto the rink.

If the rest of those rockers were doing their thing to sixteenth notes, I was plodding along on whole notes, inching my way toward that terrifying corner. Skating straight-on wasn't so bad. In fact, I was even picking up speed. But how was I ever going to manipulate that corner? How did all those wee people make their skates turn ninety degrees?

Where are my children when I need them? I panicked, desperately searching for at least one familiar face.

It must have been natural talent just oozing out of my terrified body. Before I knew what was happening, I had automatically leaned into my left skate, pushed back with my right, and made an almost-passable turn. At least I was still going in the same direction as all the other skaters.

Although I'd been feeling like a Model-T Ford in a race with Corvettes, I felt myself starting to loosen up. Still, every one of those six-to-sixteen-year-old squirts were passing me like crazy. The only thing I could do to save face was speed up my act. So I did. I also dusted up the bottom of my pants and bruised my pride a little when I hit the floor.

Before long I realized I'd been boogie-ing on roller skates for half an hour. I was even starting to move my shoulders and hips to the beat of great classics like "Pac Man Fever" and "Stayin' Alive."

When my children finally noticed me, they screeched up to my side and actually offered to skate with me. I was shocked! Were these the same kids who didn't walk with me in department stores because it wasn't "cool" to go shopping with your mom?

Were these the same kids who ate and ran at every meal because conversing with a mom after dinner over tea was boring with a capital "B"? Now they were asking if I wanted to skate with them?

I accepted their offers gladly. Having small yet steady hands to hold boosted my confidence. I started to relax. The pain in my shins went away.

When the disk jockey announced the "Hokey Pokey," I didn't race for the concession stand. I stood firm, following his directions. I put my left leg in, my left leg out, my right leg in, my right leg out. After we hokey-pokeyed all the body parts, I was ready to rest each and every one of them.

That was about the time the disk jockey called for the backward skate session, so naturally I chickened out and used that time to treat the children to soft drinks and pretzels.

During this interlude I blabbered about how much fun I was having, how proud I was of myself, and what great "quality time" this was for all of us. My three charming diplomats nodded in agreement with bright statements like "Yeah, you're doin' OK Mom" and "Ya wanna play crack the whip?"

The only bruise on my apple that day was the walnut-sized blister I had on my foot when I got home. When I went back two weeks later, I ended up with a blister on top of a blister. But by this time I was hooked. "Quality time" had suddenly taken on a whole new meaning. Now it was something I enjoyed as much as the kids did.

These days, I'm still roller-skating, outdoors, for exercise. I look like a robot with knee and elbow pads, hand and wrist guards, but at least I'm out there, rolling on down the sidewalks of life.

Part Two:

❦

Faith Matters

TERRIFIED ON
TIMPANAGOS MOUNTAIN
~~~

During the summer of 1993, Andrew (then thirteen); Wayne, a widowed family friend; and I took a four-week trip across America. We drove over six thousand miles from Wisconsin to California and back.

We saw flooded Iowa, the fields of Nebraska, Wyoming ranches, miles of white salt flats in Utah, gigantic domed rocks in Yosemite, and sea lions splashing in the Pacific Ocean. We zoomed down a three thousand-foot alpine slide in the rugged, snow-topped mountains along the Continental Divide in Colorado; drove through the Black Hills and the Badlands; drank free ice water at Wall Drug; marveled at South Dakota's Corn Palace; and tried to count the lakes in Minnesota. It was an amazing adventure. But the most memorable moment of our trip happened on Timpanogos Mountain outside Salt Lake City, Utah.

On a warm, sunny July afternoon, Wayne's van chugged up the foothills of the Timpanogos Mountains. When we reached the place where you buy tickets for the cave tour near the top of the mountain, we saw a sign:

> To reach Timpanogos Cave, visitors must hike the 1.5 mile cave trail. This hard-surfaced trail rises 1,065 feet and is considered a STRENUOUS HIKE. Anyone with heart trouble or walking or breathing problems should not attempt the hike. Allow three hours for the round trip, including an hour in the cave. Individuals under 16 must be supervised by an adult at all times.

Since it was just after 3 P.M., we had plenty of time before dark to walk up the trail, catch the last cave tour of the day, and hike back down. We bought our tickets and started to climb.

Even though we were in pretty good shape, that trail was so steep we were huffing and puffing not long after we began. Every quarter mile or so we'd sit down on a bench to catch our breath. Enormous pines hundreds of feet below, sheer cliffs, rocks that stretched to the heavens, and a clear blue sky that went on forever, greeted us at every rest. Finally, after an hour of exhaustive climbing, we reached the entrance to the cave.

I plopped down on a bench just inside the cave entrance. I was seated next to an older man wearing a one-piece beige worksuit and a miner's hat with a light attached. I tried to make conversation but he looked at me as if he didn't understand what I was saying, then finally spoke in a very thick Spanish accent.

I asked him to repeat himself. Finally I understood. It had taken him over two and a half hours to climb up the mountain. He was exhausted and upset that he'd missed the scheduled time for his tour. His name was Emilio and he was originally from Madrid, Spain. He was sixty-nine years old and said he had no idea how steep the climb would be before he started.

Then our tour guide appeared. She welcomed Emilio into our group and opened the door to the cave.

An hour and a half later, after exploring the beautiful, winding Timpanogos caves, we stepped back into the daylight. Only it wasn't bright and sunny like before. It was cloudy and windy and starting to sprinkle.

Andrew didn't like the looks of it one bit.

"Mom, hurry up, it's raining. We gotta get down. It could be a big storm."

I glanced behind me toward the cave exit, wondering what was taking Emilio so long. I stalled a bit by walking over to the guest register and signing our names. Normally, I would have dashed off with Andrew and Wayne and rushed down the mountain, but on that day, something unusual happened. I can't explain it other than to say that a voice inside my head said I needed to wait for Emilio.

"Mom! Come on. Look at how windy it's getting! We gotta get down!"

"Andrew, wait a minute. Emilio's right behind us."

"Who cares? Mom, it's really starting to rain! Let's go!"

Even Wayne tried to get me to hurry up, but I didn't listen to him, either. I had no idea what was ahead of us or why I couldn't leave without the old man, but that inner voice would not let me leave until Emilio was safely out of the cave and walking with us.

I tried to reason with Andrew and Wayne. "Come on, guys, it's going to take us at least an hour to get down. We're going to get wet no matter what. Let's just wait for Emilio."

"But, Mom, see those black clouds over Salt Lake City in the distance? That's rain pouring out of them! And they're moving this way! It's getting darker!"

I could see my son was really scared. I certainly didn't like what I saw ahead of us either. A steep, narrow mountain path with no guard rail was *not* where I wanted to be during a thunderstorm.

Just then Emilio stepped out of the cave. Wayne and Andrew skittered down the first leg of the switchback path. I walked slowly, just ahead of Emilio. Within a few minutes Andrew and Wayne had disappeared around the first sharp turn.

"Mom! Hurry up!" Andrew yelled. "I can see lightning in the distance!"

Just then a giant sharp cracking noise slammed into the mountain. It wasn't the rolling thunder I was used to in Wisconsin. This sounded like ten thousand bullwhips had snapped right in front of us into the side of the rock, a nasty heart-stopping sound. Then a giant rod of white light zig-zagged just ahead of us.

"Mom!" Andrew screamed. "Hurry up!" I knew my son wanted to run and not stop until he reached the bottom where the car was.

The wind roared and I crouched behind a rock outcrop. As the sky turned black, the clouds let loose and the pouring rain began. Stones and small rocks flew off the mountain and dropped at our feet. I could feel my heart slamming against my chest. I closed my eyes tight and prayed as more lightning flashed in front of us.

"Ouch!" Andrew yelped. "Mom, I just got hit in the head by a rock the size of a baseball! Can't you go any faster?"

I couldn't move. I started praying again: *God, don't let us die out here! Protect Emilio and keep his legs strong.*

For the first time in my life, I honestly thought I might die. I thought we would all die. *Maybe it's our time,* I reasoned. I figured at best we'd get struck by lightning and die instantly. At worst the wind would blow us off the path and we'd plunge down the steep rocky thousand-foot drop to the valley below.

Wayne was up ahead trying to cover his eyes from the thick dust blowing around our heads. He pulled up the hood on his sweatshirt and crouched down to wait for me. Andrew pulled his baseball cap further down on his head as the rain soaked his t-shirt. I pulled my reading glasses out of my pocket, shouting over the wind, "I have to wear these or I can't see! There's too much dust blowing in my eyes! Stay calm, guys, we're going to be OK."

Another giant crack. This one sounded like the mountain itself had split in half. Then more lightning, closer this time.

Wayne and Andrew were fifty feet ahead of Emilio and me. There were places on the path that had a blue line painted down the middle. A sign said that when you saw a blue line you were supposed to walk fast because those were the areas where rock slides were likely to occur. Wayne and Andrew were on one side of a rock slide area, Emilio and I were on the other.

I was shivering as cold rain ran down my neck. Finally, I looked up to make sure no large rocks were falling and raced across the blue line section and caught up to Wayne and Andrew.

"We have to wait for Emilio," I said matter-of-factly.

"Why, Mom? He can make it by himself. He got up here, didn't he? I don't like this. Let me go by myself! You know how long it took Emilio to get up this mountain! I can't stand this!"

I put my hands on Andrew's shoulders. "Andrew, please. He's not very strong. He just told me he was in the hospital last summer with an ulcerated pancreas. His knees hurt him, Andrew. It's harder walking down this mountain than it was going up. I'm using muscles I've never used before to keep from falling on my face! And now the path is wet and slippery. It's covered with rocks and there's no guard rail."

Crack! Another thunderclap. A huge bolt of lightning followed almost immediately. I took a deep breath and grabbed a tree root sticking out of the side of the mountain for support.

"What? I can't hear you!" Andrew shouted hysterically.

I had to yell over the howling wind, "Andrew, think of all the things that could happen to Emilio. He could lose his balance and slip on a rock. He could have a heart attack from the exhaustion. He…"

Andrew pulled away from me and interrupted. "OK, OK! Geez, Mom, this is going to take forever!" He wasn't happy but I think he was starting to understand.

"Wait Andrew, I'm not finished."

Andrew rolled his eyes, expecting a lecture. I put my hands back on his shoulders. Suddenly, once again, a voice spoke inside my head, *Use Andrew's shoulders.*

"Andrew, you're strong. I can feel it in your shoulders. You're five feet, nine inches, a little shorter than Emilio. How would you feel about letting him put his hands on your shoulders from behind for support?"

I looked back up the path at Emilio. I could see clumps of wet white hair under the child-sized miner's cap he'd purchased earlier that day in the gift shop below. He was bent over, hands on his knees, panting for breath. I looked at the dark clouds. It was still raining and the path was sloppy wet and slippery. Andrew was looking at him too... then at the black clouds, at the bent trees blowing wildly in the wind, and then back at Emilio.

Then his voice softened, "OK, Mom. I'll do it."

Emilio liked the idea of using Andrew's shoulders for support as the two of them "baby-stepped" down the path as the rain pelted their backs. Shuffle, rest. Shuffle, rest. Emilio could only take twenty or so steps before he had to lean against the mountain and rest his knees.

Gradually the wind died down enough that we could hear each other talk. When the path got really steep, Andrew placed his hands on Wayne's shoulders. With Emilio's hands on Andrew's shoulders, they looked like the blind leading the blind leading the blind. Andrew thought they looked so funny that he started whistling the song from *Bridge on the River Kwai* where the prisoners did their single-file death march. In a few seconds Wayne, Emilio, and I were all whistling along with him.

Then Emilio started teaching Andrew Spanish. "Ésta es una montaña grande. ¡Vamos amigos!" He'd say phrases in Spanish and Andrew would repeat them.

Next he told Andrew tales about his life in Madrid, his Cuban wife, how he'd lived in New York for many years, and the three years he worked as an auditor on a Norwegian ship.

As I walked ahead, kicking stones and rocks out of the path, I could tell from Andrew's comments and questions that he was genuinely starting to like this old guy. Even when they had to stop every few minutes to give Emilio's knees a rest, they joked back and forth until we'd hear Emilio's loud voice echo through the mountains, "¡Vamos muchachos!"

After an hour the black clouds moved further south. Our slow procession continued as the pounding rain gradually slowed to a drizzle. For three and a half hours as we four inched our way down that steep, slippery path, Emilio and Andrew were glued to each other, Emilio's hands on Andrew's shoulders.

Ten feet before we reached the bottom, Emilio pulled away from my son and stood tall by himself. In his loud, clear voice with the thick Spanish accent, he proclaimed, "I do the last steps myself! So, Wayne, when we reach the bottom, shall we purchase the tickets to do this again tomorrow?" he laughed.

We all laughed. When Emilio reached level ground we cheered. I gave him a hug and we walked him to his car in the dark of night. By now it was after 9:30 P.M., and our two cars were the only ones left in the parking lot.

Before he opened his car door, Emilio shook Andrew's hand and said, "Andrew, you are a fine young man. I could not have made it down without your help. Thank you."

Later, as we drove back to Salt Lake City, Andrew said he felt sad when Emilio drove away. He said he wanted to talk to him some more, that he wanted to hear his big belly laugh again.

I asked Andrew if he'd learned anything special that day. He thought for a minute, then smiled. "Yup. I learned that when you help somebody you forget your own fears. From that first minute when Emilio put his hands on my shoulders, I wasn't afraid of the storm anymore. I also learned that God definitely answers your prayers. When we weren't talking or whistling, I was praying... a lot."

MICHAEL'S MOUTH

When Michael was eight years old, we moved from the small town of Rock Falls, Illinois to Oak Creek, Wisconsin, a suburb of Milwaukee, the state's largest city. Michael and his two older sisters were pulled out of a small, cozy Catholic grade school—the same one I'd attended as a child—and placed in a large, bustling public school.

After a few months I heard reports from the two older girls that Michael had picked up some language on the playground that was a little rough around the edges. Michael and I had a heart-to-heart talk in the living room. He seemed impressed with the give-and-take discussion and promised to watch his mouth.

A few months later Michael's oldest sister, Jeanne, came in from a rousing snowball fight with her pesky brother. "Michael has a garbage mouth! You should have heard what he said to me, Mom!"

Time for another heart-to-heart talk in the living room. This time a punishment seemed in order. After a lecture on the advantages of talking like a gentleman, one of which was being allowed to remain a member of the family, I said, "Michael, I think you should write a two-hundred-word essay on 'Why God gave me a mouth.'"

Have you ever seen an eight-year-old boy's face fall as far as his sneakers? His shoulders sagged and his whole body dragged as he slumped off to his room to begin the torture of writing two hundred words.

What emerged on that paper a couple of hours later made up for all the teasing, horseplay, and grumbling Michael had ever done in his young life—and for the street language, too. His essay, in my eyes, was a prize-winning masterpiece... and I told him so. In fact, feeling a little guilty after giving him the punishment in the first place for fear he'd grow up to hate writing, I praised him to the skies and encouraged his writing skills from that day on.

Here is part of his magical essay.

"Why God Gave Us a Mouth"

God gave us mouths so we would be able to eat the fine food He gave us like fish, bread, and peanut butter and jelly on white bread. He also gave us a mouth so we would be able to blow bubbles for your baby brother or sister. And so we could sing in His beautiful house, the church. He also gave us a mouth so if we were working we could whistle and that would make us work faster because we wouldn't be so bored.

God gave us a mouth so we could smile and frown but mostly to smile. God gave us a mouth so we could say sorry when we get in a fight with somebody. God gave us a mouth so we could talk and reason with people before they really get us for it. God gave us a mouth so we could say, "I love my parents!" Love, Michael.

P.S. I'm Sorry!!!

Michael's punishment essay didn't quite capture the reason why we shouldn't use foul language, but it did express many of the reasons we can all be thankful God gave us a mind, a voice, and a heart big enough to say, "I'm sorry." God also gave us a little boy named Michael, and for this I'll be eternally grateful.

"Seed Faith Money"

～

One thing I've learned over the years as a single parent is to pay close attention to other single parents. Watch how they handle things. See how they cope. And if what they're doing seems to work better than what you're doing, go for it!

You've probably already met someone whose faith is so deep that it just sort of rubs off on you a little. For me, Rosemary was one of those people.

I met Rosemary when she came to Wisconsin to visit Sharon, one of her dearest friends from college. Sharon is also one of my closest friends, so the three of us got together.

Rosemary talked about 1984, one of the scariest years of her life. Newly divorced, she was overwhelmed by the awesome responsibility of raising two daughters alone. There were many weeks when she had less than $50 to her name. No matter how hard she tried, she said she always seemed to be one card short of a full deck when it came to money.

At Easter time in 1986 Rosemary's daughter Theresa discovered a pea-sized lump on her collarbone. After numerous X-rays and blood work, the tests showed that she had an L-shaped Hodgkin's disease tumor filling 40 percent of her chest cavity.

In addition to the terror of watching Theresa suffer, Rosemary was also distraught over the enormous medical bills that were piling up. Her insurance paid 80 percent, but the other 20 percent caused her seesawing finances to plunge off the deep end. At one point she owed the hospital and doctors $1,500.

A few weeks later, quite unexpectedly, Rosemary was named "Employee of the Year" for the Department of Commerce's Pacific Fisheries Service and received a prize of $1,500: exactly the amount she needed. *What a stroke of luck!* Rosemary thought.

At church that Sunday a voice overpowered her inner being so loud and clear that she had to shake her head to make sure she wasn't dreaming. The voice said, "Give Maggie $100."

"What?" Rosemary demanded a repeat.

"Give Maggie $100."

"Maggie? The Maggie whose job I took over when she quit at the Fisheries Service?" She was the only Maggie that Rosemary knew.

There it was again. A voice from somewhere, telling her to give this woman a hundred dollars.

"Why does this woman need me to give her $100?" Rosemary asked the voice. "And who is this, anyway? Why are you asking me to do this? I'm the one struggling financially! At least Maggie has a husband to help her!"

Rosemary thought about her recent windfall. After tithing and paying taxes on it, the amount she actually cleared from that prize was less than a thousand dollars. Not even enough to cover the medical bills. And now someone—*was it God himself?* Rosemary wondered—was asking her to give $100 to a woman she hardly knew!

"This is ridiculous," she said to herself. "Give $100 to Maggie? Why, it's total fiscal irresponsibility!"

At home that afternoon Rosemary kept hearing the voice, "Give Maggie $100."

She dug deep into her faith reserve and remembered the verse from Matthew 28:20 that says, "Behold, I am with you always, even to the end of the world."

Rosemary thought back to the last few months of Theresa's struggle with Hodgkin's disease. By now she was well on the road to complete recovery. She hadn't even gotten sick from the chemotherapy. Yes, God had been with them throughout the whole ordeal, but Rosemary also knew that God doesn't ask for paybacks.

No, it didn't make sense, but she reached for her checkbook.

Shaking and sweating, she wrote the check and mailed it to Maggie.

A week later Maggie stood on Rosemary's doorstep. Smiling, Maggie handed the check back. "I can't accept this, Rosemary. But I want you to know that you certainly did God's work when you sent it. My husband was getting so bitter about God and religion. He was so touched by your generosity. He's acting like a whole new person. Thank you so much," she beamed as she pressed the $100 check back into Rosemary's hand.

That Sunday Rosemary tithed an extra $10 for the $100 Maggie had given back to her. On Monday, Rosemary received a check in the mail from her Aunt Joey for $100 for no particular reason... something her aunt had never done before.

On Tuesday, Rosemary tithed $10 of that money to the church. On Friday she received a $100 check in the mail from her good friend, Sharon, who enclosed a note that said simply, "I'm sure you can use this." Sharon had never done such a thing before.

That's when it hit Rosemary square in the eye. "When God asked me to give Maggie $100 for no apparent reason, I'd listened, a bit grudgingly, I'll admit. Was it a test, like when God instructed Abraham to sacrifice Isaac, his beloved son? And just as God had spared Isaac at the last minute, he spared me by bringing that $100 back to me three times in six days!"

In the fall of 1990, Rosemary's finances were again extremely grim. Her older daughter Claire was getting ready to go back to college, and Rosemary was frantic over how she would come up with the money for her tuition.

"I had some antique jewelry that had been given to me years earlier. I didn't want to sell it, but keeping in mind how, in the past, when I put my faith in God—*by now I was sure the voice was God's*—somehow financial matters fell into neat, well-tended rows. So I took a deep breath and sowed more seeds of trust.

"That's when it happened. The voice. The same one that bombarded me in church when I was told to give $100 to Maggie. Only this time it said, 'Give $100 to Margaret.'"

Rosemary says she almost wailed out loud as she thought to herself, *Now just a minute! I took a loss on the jewelry when I sold it, because I have faith in you! And you're STILL asking me to give Margaret $100?*

Margaret, a struggling single parent, was sitting next to Rosemary in church that Sunday. Rosemary knew it was useless to argue: "The world says 'hang onto your money.' But sometimes God says, 'give it away.'"

She gave Margaret the $100.

Within five days the bank suddenly approved an "iffy" college loan that would help with Claire's tuition. And the following week Rosemary received a very nice and quite unexpected raise at work.

The next week in church she quieted herself and prepared to "listen" to what God had in mind for her now… more out of curiosity at the absurdity of it all than eagerness, she admits. Within a few minutes she was directed to give another struggling single parent whom she barely knew $150.

Rosemary says she may have given it one final "Aw, come on, God, you've got to be kidding!" But by this time she was a believer. She'd been taught over and over that if she just puts out seedling effort, God returns his bounty in bushels.

Just before I met Rosemary, she almost gave up her hobby of writing to over a hundred friends from grade school, high school, and college, as well as former neighbors in Wisconsin, Colorado, and California… because of rising postage costs. But she refused to worry about it. Sharing her "seed faith money" stories and other examples of Christ's work in her life with her friends seemed more important than worrying about postage costs.

And so Rosemary continued to tithe and then simply put her finances on a limb and sent out a mailing with her last few "postage" dollars.

A few days later she received an unsigned Easter card. When she opened it a $100 bill fell out.

Rosemary explains it all quite simply. "As long as I give back to God a portion of what God has given to me, I'm free! No more worries. Besides, when you really listen for the voice of God, it's amazing what you hear."

OUTSIDE THE CIRCLE OF POSSIBILITY

~~~

"Hey Mom! I'm going to apply to this student exchange program to study art in a foreign country this summer."

I nearly dropped the plates I was carrying to the dining room table. "Oh sure," I quipped, "and I think I'll apply to be a belly dancer in Nepal for the summer."

"Mom, this is serious. My friend Heather went to Germany last summer. Think of the experience!"

"Jeanne, you're sixteen years old. Besides, foreign exchange programs are for rich kids. They cost thousands of dollars. Have you forgotten that I'm a single parent with three other children to worry about besides you, and that I'm already working three part-time jobs? Please, honey, be reasonable."

The next day Jeanne sent in her application to Open Door Student Exchange in New York. An enthusiastic art student at the Milwaukee High School of the Arts, she let nothing—not even a negative mother—dampen her spirits.

I just shook my head and whispered a prayer that she would not be too disappointed when she discovered we really couldn't afford to let her go to Europe for the summer.

A few weeks later when the Open Door people sent her another longer application to fill out, I read the paragraph that said, "Comprehensive fee of $2,750 covers international airfare, orientation, room and board, insurance, activities, materials, excursions, counseling, and administrative support for the six-week summer program."

Three thousand dollars, including airfare to New York and back. *Impossible!* I thought. *How can she be so bold as to even think that I could consider this*? I tossed the application on the counter and went back to the kitchen sink to peel potatoes.

A few days later Jeanne told me she'd filled out the second application and mailed it.

My heart ached for her and I started to hate my single-parent status even more.

"Jeanne, you know we can't afford it. Besides, you don't know anything about traveling in a foreign country. You don't even speak a foreign language. At least wait until you're in college to dream something this big."

"Mom, I HAVE to apply. I'll never know if I can go if I don't try."

Something rang true in her words. Was it the unfaltering optimism I'd always had myself until single parenthood shook me into a sense of gloom and doom?

A few weeks later I received a phone call from Open Door in New York. "Mrs. Lorenz, we received Jeanne's application for the summer program abroad, but she didn't send the application fee."

I politely told the young woman that I couldn't afford the application fee and that spending summer in a foreign country was out of the question financially for my daughter. I explained that I had recently become a single parent and that paying my bills and getting by day to day was my main concern. "Even with a thousand-dollar scholarship, I still couldn't afford to let her go," I told the woman.

Two months later the vice-president of the student exchange program called me at work. "Mrs. Lorenz, we were so impressed with Jeanne's application that we've called some of her teachers to find out more about her. She would certainly benefit from our fine art workshop in Cologne, West Germany, this summer. The deadline for final applications is past and we have some scholarship money left. Can you tell me exactly what you *could* afford?"

I sighed, wondering if these people would ever get off my back. Almost facetiously I mentioned a paltry sum that I'd saved for emergencies, something in the neighborhood of $300.

"We'll make up the difference with scholarship and grant money," Mr. Lurie responded. "Start the preparations for getting Jeanne a passport."

Was it possible? I wondered in a daze. I worried. I prayed. How could such a dream come true? I remembered reading something in the Bible about reaching for the impossible.

For if you had faith even as small as a tiny mustard seed you could say to this mountain, "Move!" and it would go far away. Nothing would be impossible.   **Matthew 17:20**

I wondered where my daughter had acquired such a sense of bulldozing faith.

I called Jeanne's art teachers and asked what they thought about sending her to Cologne for the summer.

"What an opportunity!" they shouted into the phone. "Cologne is one of the art centers of the world! Let her go!"

That afternoon I made a huge sign that said "Bon Voyage, Jeanne" and taped it to the front door. When she arrived home from school she screamed, danced around the kitchen, smeared away her happy tears, then hugged me hard.

When I met my daughter at the airport at the end of the summer after her adventure abroad, I saw a young woman who was different than the daughter I'd kissed goodbye six weeks earlier.

She'd had the most incredible experience of her life. The first three weeks, during the intensive art history/sketching course, she'd lived in a youth hostel. Then she stayed with an architect, his wife, and their two children. Mr. Schweizer loved art passionately and was delighted to have a house guest who shared his enthusiasm.

The Schweizers showered Jeanne with trips to museums,

cathedrals, and travels to other German cities to see examples of Gothic, Romanesque, and Baroque art and architecture. She soaked up the culture of Germany, the homeland of our Kobbeman and Lorenz ancestors. She returned to America with a new sense of pride in her own country with its diverse cultures. Most of all, she returned with a sense of confidence in dreaming big dreams.

After she came home Jeanne spent the next few months applying to various colleges and universities. Even though she received an art scholarship to the University of Wisconsin, she also applied to spend a year in Yugoslavia through the Open Door Student Exchange. She was accepted for the program after learning that the U.S. Information Agency was giving each of the fifteen American students going to Yugoslavia a $2,000 grant... which again brought the program into our reach financially. Without hesitation Jeanne decided to postpone college for a year.

So once again, an incredible foreign experience opened up for the child of a single parent who never in a million years believed that overseas education opportunities were within her reach.

Today, as I look at my daughter—who has since graduated from college and is a successful artist and teacher—I remember her faith in the impossible when, as a sixteen-year-old high school student, she wanted more than anything to visit a foreign country. I see how much she matured and learned from her experiences in Germany and Yugoslavia, and I know that for the rest of her life, the same faith will pull her through.

That Bible verse about moving mountains, taped over my kitchen sink, is a daily reminder to keep my heart open and to believe that, no matter how many obstacles there are, I can still reach for a star. Because when I do there's a very good chance that I'll receive a whole galaxy in the process.

A TALE OF TWO TEENS

When I read the front page story in the *Milwaukee Journal* on November 7, 1989, I felt like someone had tossed cold water on me. The story had been written by a columnist from the *Minneapolis Star Tribune*, Al Sicherman.

"JOE WAS BRIGHT—HE WOULD NOT DO DRUGS."

Dear, dear friends: This isn't going to be easy. My older son, Joe, of whom I was very, very proud, and whose growing up I've been privileged to chronicle occasionally in the newspaper, died last month in a fall from the window of his seventh-floor dorm room in Madison, Wisconsin. He had taken LSD. He was eighteen.

I kept reading as thoughts of my own teenagers flashed across my mind. Jeanne, a college freshman in California; Julia, a college freshman at the University of Wisconsin, Stevens Point; Michael, a high school senior, heading for the University of Wisconsin-Madison in the fall of 1990. *All three of them good, bright kids like Joseph Sicherman,* I thought. *How could this happen to a good kid like that?* The article about Joe continued.

He must not have known how treacherous LSD can be. I never warned him because, like most adults, I had no idea it was popular again. I thought it had stopped killing kids twenty years ago. Besides, Joe was bright and responsible. He wouldn't 'do' drugs. It didn't occur to me that he might dabble in them.

I thought back over the past few years. I thought about my divorce and the hard time I had adjusting to single parenthood. When my husband moved out, the four children were in four different schools. The logistics of keeping all that organized by myself left little time for talking about drugs.

Besides, I rationalized, *they know how I feel. I won't even allow my friends to smoke cigarettes in our home! Isn't that a powerful enough message to give my children about drugs?* I wondered.

I knew Julia had had a few beers with her friends when she was in high school. I remembered the day she and her friends snuck down to the creek for an impromptu "party" after school one spring day.

When I found out about the drinking, I ranted, raved, preached, scorned, and warned. I did all the usual things parents do when their kids break the law. I pointed my finger and left a very clear message: "There will be no drinking as long as you're living under my roof!" And then I prayed.

The summer before Julia left for college was a rough one. She was impatient, sassy, and uncooperative. I'd remind her to start getting things organized for college. She'd ignore me. Then out of the blue she'd snap about something or other. If I didn't snap back, I'd just shake my head and walk away. After a few shouting matches I secretly started counting the days till she would be leaving.

The day before we left for Stevens Point, Julia met me at the door when I came home from work. "Mom, I did it! Everything's packed and ready to be put in the car. My room's in perfect order! I even cleaned up the family room."

Maybe things will work out with Julia after all, I thought. I'd arranged a day off work so I could take her to college, help her unpack, and then spend the night in a hotel with her so we could have some quality "mother/daughter" time to make up for the roller coaster feelings of the past summer.

The weekend went beautifully. We toured the campus, met some of the girls in her dorm, had fun arranging "her half" of the room, and ended the weekend with a special dinner at a Chinese restaurant. It was hard to say goodbye when I had to leave, but I knew she was ready for college; I had two sons at home who needed my attention. When I pulled away after telling her I loved her, I said something trite like "Remember, you're in college to study. Stay away from the wild parties."

Driving the three hours home alone that evening wasn't nearly as depressing as I thought it would be. I remember thinking *Julia will be fine. Well, at least I don't have to worry about her anymore. Two kids down, two to go.*

Two months later when I was reading the article about Joe Sicherman, I wondered if I'd really made an impression on Julia about drugs and alcohol. Had we ever really talked about it? Had she listened? Had she told me *her* real feelings about drugs? Had I listened?

Al Sicherman wrote, "I didn't take Joe for granted.... But I certainly took his life for granted. Parents must not do that. We must be scared for them. They don't know when to be scared for themselves."

I picked up the phone to call Julia. I had to warn her about drugs again. I wanted her to read about Joseph Sicherman.

Julia promised that she would buy a copy of the Milwaukee newspaper and read the story. Three days later I received a long typewritten letter from her.

At first I thought it was an essay she'd written for English class, but it wasn't. It was written for me. I think she also wrote it for herself.

The day I told my mother goodbye was the start of my adult life. I walked back to my dorm room and sat in silence as I reminisced about how much I struggled through high school to be free. I remember thinking that I did not work up to my full potential or my mother's high standards. I didn't get straight A's, nor was I on the honor roll, like my brother. I didn't excel in the fine arts like my sister, and at times I didn't even act right. These feelings caused me to feel below average as a student and a daughter. When I was accepted to the

University of Wisconsin at Stevens Point I decided to prove I was better than my reputation of being "average." I wanted to impress my mom, get good grades in college, and excel in other areas as well. During the first few weeks of college, I met new friends, enjoyed my classes, and became involved in dorm functions and other activities on campus. In the process of trying to become self-reliant and to be accepted among my new friends, I also managed to make a big mistake. The next part of my story is not easy to tell.

On September 21, 1989 I was fined for the consumption of alcoholic beverages and for obstructing an officer. Like the typical college freshman I wanted to go out, meet new friends, and have some fun. I went to a small house party where a friend offered me a beer. I took it. And then another. And possibly another, I'm not sure.

The next thing I remember, I was jumping out a bathroom window. The police had been called to the party and during the investigation they lined everyone up to get our names and addresses. I asked permission to go to the bathroom and jumped out the window trying to escape the nightmare that was playing in slow motion before me. I tried to run but when I came around the corner there was a policeman sitting in a squad car in front of the house. In court the next week I had to pay $72 for underaged drinking and $156 for resisting arrest.

That happened two months ago. It took me two months to regain the strength I needed to tell you my story. I am ashamed of what I did and every time I think about it I feel as though I am being slapped across the face.

I don't know how to say 'I'm sorry' but I am. I know that I only hurt myself. I am the one who is financially burdened by this and I am the one who must live with the decisions I made that night.

After reading the article you asked me to read about Joe Sicherman, the boy who jumped out a window while strung out on LSD, I found a similarity in our stories and it gave me the courage to tell you what I had done.

Joe and I were both college freshmen. Instead of using LSD, I chose alcohol. We both jumped out of a window. He lost his life, I lost $228 *and my self-respect. Going off to college, trying to fit in and have fun, while at the same time trying to do well and impress my mother, caused a situation that I lost control of, as did Joe. With the help of God and my friends I have managed to move on. I can no longer live in the past. The fines are paid and I have learned more from this experience than anything I have ever learned. Like Joe Sicherman's rabbi said at his graduation party last year, 'All things pass into mystery.' I love you. Julia."*

When I received her letter, I phoned Julia immediately. We cried together. I told her I was proud of her for being mature enough to learn from her mistake. I sent her a bouquet of flowers, as much for Joe Sicherman as for her.

After I hung up the phone, I thought about how many articles I'd read and news reports I'd seen about how drugs and alcohol are killers. I thought about the parents of teenagers who, like me, get frustrated over the shouting matches and the battle of wits that often occur between parents and teens before our children finally fray the apron strings and gain their independence. I thought about how hard it is to actually sit down with them and talk about drugs.

I thought about Jeanne and Julia and Michael, and I knew that the one thing I had to do for them was to keep talking to them about drugs, including alcohol, every time they were home from college. I did it, not just for their own good, but as a tribute to Al Sicherman in memory of his son, Joe, who "wanted to try LSD just once, just to see what it was like."

OPTIMISTICALLY SPEAKING

It was one of those long-distance phone calls every mother dreads, whether she's a single parent or not. The phone call where you immediately know something's wrong before your child even says a word after that first quiet, "Hi, Mom."

"Mom, I know these are words you never wanted to hear from one of your unmarried daughters, but here goes. I'm pregnant."

"Oh, Julia." It was all I could muster as tears filled my eyes and a baseball-size lump lodged in my throat. My mind raced. How could she have let this happen? How would she support a child? Would she be able to finish college? Julia was about to start her senior year at the University of Wisconsin-Stevens Point. This news couldn't have come at a worse time. I responded the only way I could think of: "What are you going to do?"

"Mom, women have choices these days that people didn't have when you were my age. But you know I would never have an abortion. And I could never give my baby up for adoption. This is MY baby—I'm this baby's mother! I know I made a mistake. And I'm very sorry about that. I know my timing is lousy. But, Mother, I can't undo it. I can either be miserable during this pregnancy and feel sorry for myself, or I can accept it and make the best of the situation. You've struggled raising four kids as a single parent. And you did great. You're a survivor, Mom. So am I. I can do it." Julia finally took a breath.

At that moment I wondered if my daughter would move home during the pregnancy. Would she need my help financially? Before I could ask the question, Julia continued.

"Mom, I'm going to stay in school. I have to graduate. I know I can get financial help from some government programs during the semester the baby's born."

As I listened to my daughter, it became obvious that she had already made up her mind to do this on her own. At that moment I was sure Julia could handle being an unwed mother. I knew she'd find a way to finish her senior year in college, that she'd graduate and make a good life for her child and herself.

Then I remembered. Julia wasn't the only parent of this child.

"What about Tim? Are you thinking about getting married? How does he feel?" I'd only seen Tim on two or three occasions and I didn't really know a whole lot about him.

"Tim's been wonderful. You know how much he loves kids, Mom." I didn't know, but Julia kept gushing. "Tim's mom thinks we should get married next month. She's already reserved a park for the reception, and she said her relatives would fix all the food."

A baby and now a wedding? It was all happening too fast. I listened with only a few "I see's" and "uh-huh's" punctuating my end of the conversation.

The next day Julia called me again. This time she sounded a little depressed.

"Mom, I'm so confused. Tim's mother, she means well, but she's arranging everything. Do you think we should get married? I just don't know. Right now all I can think about is the baby. Getting married, that's, well, I just don't know. I've got to finish school. It's too much at once! What do you think?"

"Do you really want to get married now?" I asked.

"Not really."

"You've only known Tim six months. Six months ago you were both in love with other people. Are you sure, absolutely sure, that Tim is the man you want to spend the rest of your life with? Marriage is a very big commitment. If you're not ready, don't do it. Having a baby and choosing your life's partner are two different things. You should have chosen your life's partner first, my dear, but now, well... perhaps you and Tim just need some time to make sure you're right for each other. In the meantime, let Tim help you with the pregnancy, emotionally and financially."

"I really want to wait until after the baby's born and after I graduate to get married. I love Tim, but you're right, we need more time to really get to know each other."

I didn't agree with Julia and Tim's next big decision, but when your child is almost twenty-two years old, you don't have much say in how they do things. Julia and Tim rented a tiny apartment off campus together and moved their meager belongings in just before classes started in the fall.

Julia finished the first semester of her senior year with good grades and continued to work a couple of part-time jobs to make ends meet. The government's WIC Program (women, infants, and children) helped by providing some high-protein pregnancy foods. Tim handed Julia his entire paycheck each week because, as he put it, "she's a bill-paying wizard."

Julia and Tim enrolled in classes through the campus ministry program to prepare Julia for Confirmation and Tim for Baptism in the Catholic Church. He wanted to be baptized the same day as his baby. They also took childbirth classes at the local hospital.

Everything seemed to be going along smoothly. I'd shared the news of Julia's pregnancy and plans to finish college before she married in my Christmas letter to out-of-town friends and relatives. My sister and sister-in-law were planning a baby shower for Julia. Dad brought the family crib to my house, "now that you're going to be a grandma," he joked.

As January rolled around and Julia's March due date came closer I felt that we were all surviving this "blip" in the dreams I'd had for each of my children. But mid-month my bubble burst when a letter arrived from an old family friend in Arizona.

Having read the news about Julia in my Christmas letter, my octogenarian friend wrote:

Julia's generation ignores the Ten Commandments and all sense of sin. But for you, Pat, to condone her living out of wedlock until she graduates is astounding. Do you still call yourself a Christian and make no attempt to impress on her the error of her ways? To write that everything is great is to kid yourself.

I felt like I'd been slapped across the face and told to stand in the corner. I read the harsh letter over and over. I wanted to cry. I asked myself, *How can I force my religious feelings on my twenty-two-year-old adult daughter? Should I have turned my back on her if she didn't comply to teach her a lesson?*

I read the letter again and then remembered another letter... a letter that was over fifty years old. It was the letter a father sent to his daughter at the beginning of World War II. The man, a strict Protestant and elder in the Christian Church, was filled with despair because his only daughter was engaged to a young fighter pilot named Ed—a good man, according to the father, except for the fact that Ed was Catholic.

August 8, 1942

Dear Lucile,

In regard to Ed, I have this to say. I have nothing against Ed as a man or as an American. I believe he is much better than the average of young men. I wish him all the success a true American is entitled to. You seem, however, to continue to ignore the fact that his religious world is something entirely different than your own.

The seat of the Catholic church is in Italy. It is ruled by the Pope and his chosen representatives. They are NOT democratic in their rule. They are monarchial. Mussolini is a great Catholic and our second greatest enemy. Hitler was raised a Catholic and if he wins this war he will reorganize the Catholic church and force that belief on all his slaves. Freedom and liberty will be no more.

If you become a Catholic or marry a Catholic you separate yourself from all that has gone before you in life... your home training, the hopes of your parents, the ideals of freedom, your church, in fact everything in a spiritual way that you should hold dear. You simply enter another world.

Since reading your letter I have been thinking that you ought to finish your education and get a degree. I would like to pay your way at Texas Christian University until you graduate. While there you might meet some worthy young men. Of course right now the most and the best of the young men are in the army. In any case, remember what I told you. "Don't get married until the war is over."

With much love, I am as ever,

Your father, Porter

In spite of her father's warnings, Lucile married her true love a year and a half before the war ended. She and Ed raised three children in the Catholic Church and lived a happy life together until her death in 1979.

I was the oldest of those three children, and I will always be glad my mother didn't follow her father's stern admonitions and prejudiced warnings. I'm also very grateful that my grandfather didn't turn his back on his daughter when she married her young pilot. Over the years my grandfather grew to love and respect my father with great fervor.

All I could hope when I received that letter from my friend in Arizona was that fifty years from now, my own grand-daughter will be glad that I didn't force my opinions about morality or religion on my adult daughter. And that I didn't walk out on her when she needed a loving support system more than ever before in her life.

I'd like to think that my granddaughter will learn from her mother what I learned from mine... that it's always best to follow your heart, and if you make a mistake along the way, it's better to pick up the pieces, offer a sincere "I'm sorry," ask for God's forgiveness, and then forge ahead with an attitude that blossoms with optimism and determination.

When Jesus was teaching his people during his time on earth, he said, "I demand that you love each other, for you get enough hate from the world" (John 15:17-18).

The following year I sent Julia and Tim a letter responding to Julia's complaints that they fought too much. In it I suggested that by living together outside of marriage that they had no commitment to each other, no reason to try to make it work for the long haul.

On the phone I said, "Now when you fight, you say, 'He's such a jerk. I'm so glad I'm not married to him.' But, Julia, if you *were* married, you'd say, 'what do I need to do to make this marriage work?'"

The following June, Julia and Tim were married in a small ceremony at the Newman Center chapel on campus. It hasn't been an easy marriage, but they're trying hard to make it work. And I just know that God, who is all-forgiving, is smiling at and guiding them every day.

AND THEN THERE WAS HAILEY

❦

"Hi, Grandma!" The words rattled through my brain like fireworks as I shot out of a deep sleep. "Your first grandchild arrived twenty minutes ago, just before midnight! A girl! We named her Hailey. She and Julia are doing fine! Are you coming in the morning?" Tim gushed over the phone.

I didn't sleep much that night and left early the next morning for the three-hour drive to the college town hospital where my daughter had given birth. When I arrived I wasn't prepared for what I witnessed in Julia's room. Because she was recuperating from the surgery of an emergency cesarean section, she couldn't hold her baby for very long. Tim, on the other hand, was holding, feeding, changing, and dressing his daughter with the ease of a nanny who'd been caring for infants for years.

Tim had never been around tiny babies much and certainly had never taken care of one. But there I was, witnessing the joy of unrehearsed fatherhood.

Of course I convinced this young man to let me hold and rock my granddaughter for an hour or so that morning, but he was clearly the one in charge of Hailey's care.

Julia told me later that the minute the nurses were finished with Hailey after her birth, Tim held her in his arms. For six hours from the time she was one hour old at 1 A.M. until 7 o'clock the next morning, he cradled his baby close to his beating heart without putting her down once. At one point Julia looked over and saw her macho, hockey-playing, truck-driving boyfriend crying.

Fearing that Tim was disappointed because he didn't get the son he'd bragged about and hoped for during the pregnancy, Julia asked, "Tim, are you sad she's not a boy?"

Tim looked up with surprise. "Oh no, I'm crying because I love my little daughter so much."

Julia dropped out of college that semester to stay home and take care of Hailey while Tim worked full-time at a lumber yard. During the summer Julia experienced the joy of motherhood. Her phone calls and letters to me during those months sang tales about Hailey's every little accomplishment from rolling over to smiling, about the stroller a friend loaned her so she and Hailey could go for walks, and about rummage sales where Julia found "tons of great baby clothes... and most of them were only a quarter or fifty cents!"

That summer Julia developed a sense of calmness and organization that I'd never seen in my daughter. My party-going college coed had been transformed into a mom who was spending every one of her summer days simply cherishing her new baby daughter. Not once did I hear her mention that she missed the college parties or the shenanigans with her old friends. Every conversation was about Hailey.

One day in September, after Julia started back to school to finish her senior year, she phoned. "Mom, there's a conference for people all over the United States who are experts in health promotion and wellness [Julia's major] and my professors really want me to go. The hotel where it's at is just a few miles from your house!"

Before she could even ask, I shouted into the phone, "Yes! I'd love to watch Hailey!" It would be my first full day alone with my only grandchild. I could feel a giddy sense of joy bubbling up inside.

As I watched my daughter prepare to leave her daughter the morning of the conference, I experienced that old friend "joy" once again. This time it was from watching my college-age daughter put the well-being and safety of her own child ahead of anything else in her life. I nodded enthusiastically at Julia's long list of things to do and how to do them for Hailey. I asked questions about how the stroller popped into place and how long I could play with her before she'd get sleepy.

That day was almost nonstop joy for me as I played with, strolled, talked to, laughed with, fed, took pictures of, and rocked my baby granddaughter to sleep. I checked on her every few minutes and found myself just watching her sleep, as I had done so many times when my own children were tiny.

A few weeks later Julia called me again, this time in the middle of the day with two outstanding bits of news.

"Mom, Hailey said her first word! 'Da-da!' She's saying it nonstop!" I could, indeed, hear the word "da-da" over and over, clear as a bell in the background.

"And the other thing, Mom, is that I had a long talk with the head of the department today at school. She said she can't get over how different I am this semester. She said I'm so organized and my attitude is so positive and that the entire department is amazed at how much I've accomplished and how well I'm doing in my classes."

There it was again, another surge of joy. This time it entered my system as a warm, bubbly feeling that was all jumbled up with pride and awe at the way my daughter's life was unfolding right before my eyes. I kept asking Julia questions about what else the professor had said, not wanting to let the moment slip by too quickly.

A few evenings later I phoned just to "talk" as Grandmas are prone to do. Tim answered in a very quiet voice.

"Are you there alone with Hailey?" I asked.

"Yeah, Julia's at the library studying."

"And Hailey's in your arms, right?"

"Yup. I'm watching TV and she's sleeping on my shoulder."

"So Tim, I heard Hailey said her first word."

"Sure did." He chuckled, "And it's the only word she ever needs to learn, far as I'm concerned."

I have a picture of Hailey when she was six months old in a

magnetic frame on my refrigerator. It's one of those laughing baby pictures that leaps from the paper it's printed on right into your heart. It shows a face so pure and innocent and eyes so filled with delight that her silly banana-sized grin throws big globs of joy right into the hearts of those of us who know her.

When my granddaughter was eight months old I bought a tiny blue sweatshirt, barely eight inches across the chest. I decorated it with gold fabric paint that said, "Grandma loves Hailey" and glued brightly colored puffed hearts all over the front. Making that sweatshirt, in between trips to the refrigerator to look at that laughing face, brought more joy to my life than I can possibly describe.

That year after the birth of my first grandchild, I learned that joy spills out in uproarious laughter and uncontrollable tears. I learned that joy comes from watching those you love become responsible, loving people in their own right. Knowing that Julia put another life ahead of her own at a time when she could have made her education, career, and freedom the highest priority, is the part of joy that I cherish most. Being happy is one thing. Being joyous is another. And for our family, Hailey makes all the difference.

RED JELL-O AT DAWN

When Andrew, at age eleven, asked if we could have a "ceremony" at the lake to commemorate the second anniversary of his dad's death, I didn't know what to think. He not only wanted us to watch the sunrise in silence at the shore of Lake Michigan, but he also insisted that we eat red cherry Jell-O with bananas in it while we sat in the sand.

"Jell-O? At six in the morning?" I asked incredulously.

"Mom, red Jell-O with bananas was Dad's favorite snack. We always made it together when I visited him on weekends," Andrew said.

I still had hurt feelings that Harold had filed for divorce two months into our agreed-upon year-long separation and then remarried the day our divorce was final. When he died two years later, I helped Andrew through the grieving process while trying to ignore my own feelings. Now we had to bring it all up again?

"Andrew, it's supposed to be really cold tomorrow. Couldn't you just think about your dad at home?"

"Mom, please, it'll be OK. I just want us to sit there on the sand and eat the Jell-O and think about Dad. We can dress warm and take a blanket."

I finally agreed... reluctantly.

"All right, Andrew. But we'll have to get up at 5:15 if you want to get there while it's still dark."

"No problem, Mom! I'll set my alarm. Do you think Wayne would come if I ask him?"

I wondered what Wayne, the man I'd been dating for a couple of months, would think about Andrew's plan. Wayne's wife had died just two months after Harold, and I knew Wayne was still dealing with his own grief. I didn't know if it was fair to drag him along to Andrew's strange beach ceremony.

That afternoon, Wayne stopped by the house while I was stirring the red Jell-O. Andrew launched into his plan.

"So Wayne, do you want to go? The sunrise will be great!"

"Sure, Andrew, I'm glad you asked me."

I shot Wayne a look that said, "Are you sure about this?"

The next morning I tossed an old green bedspread into Wayne's van. The Jell-O was retrieved from the refrigerator.

A few minutes later, in the pitch-dark, we arrived at Grant Park Beach in South Milwaukee, the only humans in sight. *Naturally,* I thought. *Nobody else in his right mind would be here at this time in this cold!*

Wayne and Andrew smoothed the bedspread on the sand about thirty feet from the jet-black water. We snuggled close to the front and pulled the back half up around our bodies as a windbreak.

After a few minutes Andrew's "silence" rule made me uncomfortable. But then I looked at Wayne and knew that he was thinking about the wonderful relationship he'd had with his beloved Janet, his wife of thirty-one years. And without a doubt, Andrew was thinking about Harold. About the walks they took along the lake. About the plays and concerts his father had taken him to. About their trip to Florida.

I looked at these two, concentrating on the "good" memories, and suddenly my heart softened. *Could it be that Andrew is on to something by having this ceremony?* I wondered.

I pulled the green spread tighter around me and recalled a verse in Philippians that said,

Fix your thoughts on what is true and good and right. Think about things that are pure and lovely, and dwell on the fine, good things in others. Think about all you can praise God for and be glad about. **Philippians 4:8**

I recalled the early days of my marriage to Harold: the bike rides, my attempts to teach him how to ice skate, the two wonderful trips to Arizona to visit his sister and brother and their families.

I remembered when Andrew was born, in Harold's fifty-first year, and how proud he was of his new son. Why, he'd passed out cigars the day he found out I was pregnant!

I remembered laughing when he dressed up in a crazy red plaid sportcoat and too-short orange plaid pants for "nerd day" at the high school where he was principal.

Suddenly the unhappy times in our marriage faded away as I watched a line of pink and steely blue clouds inching their way onto the horizon. All the good memories that I'd buried the day Harold moved out of our home came rushing back.

I put my arm around Andrew and he snuggled closer to me. The more I thought about Harold, the more I realized how much I missed him.

Even though it was still twenty minutes or so until the actual sunrise, the sun's intensity from below the horizon was filling the beach with an eerie sense of "almost" day. And I was filled with an eerie sense of "almost" peace.

Andrew motioned that it was time to eat the Jell-O. I took the lid off the container. When I placed a spoon into Wayne's hand, I squeezed his fingers through bulky gloves. He smiled, and I knew he understood what was going on in my mind and in Andrew's.

And so we three ate red Jell-O at dawn on the shore of Lake Michigan in a wind chill that felt close to zero degrees. But somehow I wasn't shivering. And the Jell-O tasted good.

Just as the sun popped up on the horizon in a magnificent display of color, Wayne and Andrew stood up.

"It's OK to talk now," Andrew said.

Wayne put his big arms around Andrew and held him close. "I know what you're going through, son. I loved my wife very much, just like you loved your dad. And it's a wonderful thing to take time to cherish those memories."

I stood up as the full ball of wild orange sun now rested precariously and breathtakingly beautiful on the horizon line.

"Andrew, let's walk along the shore for a few minutes."

"Good idea," Wayne smiled. "I'll go warm up the van."

And so it was that I was able to let an eleven-year-old child lead me into a strange world of ceremony and silence… where I was able to grieve openly and to "dwell on the fine, good things in others" and to praise God for everything in my life that is "true and good and right"… including a very special young son named Andrew.

HELPING A CHILD
COPE WITH DEATH

Andrew was nine years old when his father died. During the year that followed my ex-husband's death, I discovered a number of specific things that helped ease the grief process for Andrew. I also discovered, to my surprise, that during the process of helping my son grieve, my own grieving was eased considerably as well. Even though our marriage had ended two years before his death, the years we'd had together were packed with many good memories, and I learned that even ex-spouses need to grieve.

Psychologists tell us that all grieving takes time and that most people travel in and out of various stages of grief for weeks, months, sometimes even years. These stages of grief include denial, anger, bargaining, depression, and finally acceptance.

By doing the following things, Andrew and I both reached the "acceptance" stage in our grief process.

1. Encourage the child to talk frequently about the person who died by talking about the deceased in a natural, everyday kind of way. In the months after Harold died, I said almost daily, "Your dad sure would have been proud to see this report card" (or basketball game, school play, clean room). This helps the child remain comfortable talking about the person he loved without feeling that such talk might make those around him sad or uncomfortable.

2. Create a photo/memory album about the deceased as soon as possible after the death. Within a month after Harold's death, I went through a dozen family albums and took out many of the pictures of Andrew and his father from the time Andrew was twenty-four minutes old in his daddy's proud arms, to the day they celebrated Harold's sixty-first birthday in the hospital, just six weeks before he died, when Andrew was nine years old.

I put all these pictures in a large "MY DAD AND ME" album and under each picture typed a paragraph explaining the various things Andrew and his dad did together during that particular time in Andrew's life. For instance, the paragraph under the picture of Harold and Andrew sitting together in a jumbo jet describes the family vacation we took to Arizona when Andrew was four. The paragraph under the picture of Harold and Andrew sitting at the piano tells about the times Harold tried to teach him simple songs on the piano when Andrew was just a toddler.

The album also includes newspaper articles about his dad's retirement party, death notices, funeral program, and all the sympathy cards Andrew received.

Andrew's "MY DAD AND ME" book is a wonderful story of his relationship with his father, which Andrew not only shares with his friends and relatives, but which he will one day be able to share with his own children. The album is also an easy way for the good times they shared to remain clear in Andrew's mind. Too often, when a parent of a young child dies, the memories and details of events fade completely as the child grows older.

3. Show the child things that the deceased made, said, or accomplished during his or her lifetime. Andrew's father made many beautiful things out of wood for our home when Andrew was small. One day after the funeral, I took Andrew on a tour of each room, pointing out everything Harold had made. I wanted my son to have pleasant thoughts of his dad each time he saw the tea cabinet, newspaper holder, step-stool, wooden shelf, telephone table, kindling box, and so forth. Someday, when my son has a family of his own, I'll give him these handmade items to enjoy in his own home and to pass on to his children as heirlooms from their grandfather.

4. Encourage the child to ask the survivors for a small memento of the deceased. Even though Andrew had a good relationship with the woman Harold married after our divorce, he was embarrassed to ask her if he could have the St. Louis Cardinal baseball cap he'd given his dad on his last birthday. I wrote to Andrew's stepmother with the request, and she gave him not only that cap, but three others, plus Harold's favorite Road Runner belt buckle and a number of other items Andrew treasures. Usually the survivors are more than happy to know "who wants what" when it comes to keepsakes.

5. Suggest to the child that he or she "pray for" or "talk to" the deceased each night before going to sleep. After Harold's death Andrew often talked to his dad at bedtime, capsulizing his day, and sometimes asked his dad to watch him do something special the next day. These days Andrew still feels that his dad's spirit is his very own "guardian angel."

A beloved person who has left this life is only as far away as our own willingness to jog memories for a child. By doing these simple things during the grieving process, we can help not only our children, but ourselves as well, to move through the various stages of grief toward acceptance.

BACK TO CHURCH

Although my faith remained strong during the summer of 1988—just a year after my divorce was final—I started getting lazy about attending church every Sunday. It seemed easy, partially because my children were scattered that summer. Jeanne was working at a camp in Michigan. Julia worked Sundays at a local motel, cleaning rooms. Michael often worked 9-5 on Sundays at the local pharmacy. Andrew was usually at his dad and stepmother's house for the weekend. So that left John, the man I was dating at the time, and me to enjoy our Sunday mornings with the newspaper, a cup of tea, and a leisurely breakfast by ourselves on my deck. Or a chance to "find God in nature" as we put it... by taking a long Sunday morning walk.

John hadn't been to church in years, and as I began to cherish those quiet Sunday mornings with him, I wondered if going to church every single Sunday (as I had done all my life) was really important. The summer slipped by; I have to admit that I missed more Sundays than I attended.

The Sunday after Labor Day, however, eight-year-old Andrew was home asking "What time are we going to church, Mom?" It had been a hectic, getting-the-kids-back-in-school, stressful week. An hour of peace in church sounded like a refreshing idea. John even agreed to go along.

During the liturgy our pastor spoke about faith being something you have to work at by being involved. Ouch! That certainly hit me smack across my conscience. I hadn't been involved in *anything* at church for months.

As I sat there listening, I felt an overwhelming peace and a desire to get re-involved. John must have felt it too because he reached for my hand as if to say, "There's something comforting here."

After the service I talked with old friends, introduced John to our pastor, and then signed up to host a discussion group in my home. We didn't stay away after that. Instead of church feeling like an "obligation," I began to cherish the comfort, peace, and involvement of community worship.

John moved to a different state the following year, but it didn't matter. I'd rekindled old friendships and become part of church again. I felt able to move on without him.

The pastor was right: the more involved I was at church, the stronger my faith grew. The following year I even taught seventh-grade religion class. And never again did I let a summer slip by without nearly perfect attendance at church.

Sometimes when I'm in church these days and my thoughts drift to something in the outside world, I say the same prayer I said the fall of 1988 when I returned to weekly church attendance.

"This Sunday, Lord, and every Sunday, keep me in the habit of weekly worship. Help me to return, during this one hour a week, a smattering of the goodness that you lavish upon me every hour of every week, year after year."

THE GIFT GRINCH

It was dark outside, snowy, windy, and cold. Two days before Christmas and there we were schlepping up and down the aisles of Sam's Wholesale Club in Milwaukee. I was exhausted after a long day in my home office. But Andrew, a high-school freshman at the time, had insisted we make the trip.

"Come on, Mom, you have to tell me what you want for Christmas. I really want to get you something nice, something you want. I don't know what you want. Give me some hints," he pleaded.

I harrumphed, noting my headache had intensified. "Why couldn't you have thought about this three weeks ago? Or three months ago? Why couldn't you have gone to the store near our house with one of your friends and picked out something? I hate being here two days before Christmas when I've got a thousand things on my mind with all the kids coming home tomorrow. I hate having to pick out my own Christmas present. Are you going to wrap it up and expect me to act surprised when I open it in front of everyone?"

I felt hot tears piling up on the underside of my eyelids, but I blinked hard. I was *not* going to cry right there in the middle of the doggone store.

My voice trailed off when I noticed the forlorn look on my son's face. I hated myself for being such a grinch.

"I'm sorry, Andrew. I'm just tired. You know what I'd really like?"

"What?" his voice sounded positively exuberant.

"A toaster oven."

"Great! Let's look at 'em," he said as he steered me over to the small appliance section.

Madame Scrooge surfaced again. "Oh no! Look at those

prices! You can't afford $50. I won't let you spend that much. There's no need. This is stupid, Andrew. Let's go home. You don't need to get me a Christmas present."

"Mom, please, I really want to get it for you. I've got the money. I've been saving for months, and I want to get you something nice that you'll use a lot. This is perfect."

"How about if I pay for half of it? Then it'll be a gift for both of us. You'll enjoy a toaster oven as much as I will."

"No! Mom, please, I want to buy it for you. Please, let me do it."

I stopped arguing and tried to put on a happy face as Andrew paid for his purchase with mostly fives and singles. As he carried the big box to the car, I noticed he was walking taller, happier.

At home I made myself a cup of lemon tea, went down to the family room, turned on the Christmas tree lights, and flopped into my favorite rocker. *Why am I such a crab when it comes to gifts?* I wondered.

I thought back to the Christmases and other gift-giving holidays that I'd survived before Andrew's father died. I recalled all those years when Harold bought me the most ridiculous gifts any human being could possibly imagine. Like the time he gave me three huge muu-muu's, in three ghastly multi-print colors, long after muu-muu's were fashionable. Or the Christmas he bought the two of us matching sports jackets, maroon with yellow stripes, in an ugly shiny material. His was a man's size extra-large, mine a man's large. I looked like a Green Bay Packer across the back, and the sleeves crept down to my knuckles. I hated those jackets more each time he pulled them out of the closet whenever we left the house together.

The next Valentine's Day Harold came downstairs with his "I have a surprise for you" grin. Before I finished flipping the pancakes, he whisked me upstairs to see his latest declaration of love. Six pink, plastic, life-size replicas of curved index fingers were screwed into the beautiful walnut paneling in our bedroom every two feet along the wall. I looked at Harold's face to see if it was a joke. My heart raced as I started praying wildly to myself, *Oh Lord, please let it be a joke! These plastic fingers sticking out of the wall don't go with my country antiques! Please, Lord, make this April Fools' day and NOT Valentine's Day!*

I turned slowly to look at my husband. His eyes were sparkling. "See, you can hang your bathrobe on this one, your pajamas on that one, your bath towel over there, your clothes on these." His face was radiant. All I could do was nod my head and hold back the tears.

Another time Harold bought me a wool skirt, blouse, and sweater outfit from a very expensive store, but it was a style and color that made me feel thirty years older and twenty pounds heavier. I didn't have the heart to take it back since it fit, but every time I wore it to please him, I felt like a flubbery version of an old schoolmarm.

I started to dread every birthday, anniversary, Mother's Day, Christmas, and Valentine's Day because I knew Harold would either buy too many little trinkets that I didn't need and wouldn't use, or he'd spend too much money on something that wasn't my taste.

Now here I was, fifteen years later, nearly fifty years old. The three older children were grown and on their own, and I was still acting skittish and mean-tempered about this gift-giving thing with Andrew.

What is it about gifts that turn me into a grinch? I asked myself over and over that night as the Christmas tree lights twinkled in the dark family room.

I decided to see if I could find something in the Bible about "gifts." After all, the Bible is supposed to have all the answers to how we should live our lives. So I turned on the overhead lights, pulled out my concordance, and looked up "gifts."

I discovered that the word "gifts" was mentioned or referred to in the Bible 129 times. So I started reading. My favorite verse, the one I thought applied to my gift dilemma, was Matthew 23:19. "For which is greater, the gift on the altar, or the altar itself that sanctifies the gift?"

Suddenly those Christmas tree lights seemed brighter. It wasn't the gift itself that was the important part of the equation. It was the heart of the giver—the vehicle of the gift, the "altar" so to speak—that made all the difference.

Just as I finished my solitary Bible study, Andrew bounded down the family room steps with his big box all wrapped. As he placed it under the tree, he smiled. "You don't have to act surprised, Mom. I'm just really glad you're going to like it. Hey, I think *I'll* like it. I can make all kinds of things in a toaster oven, right?"

"Absolutely! Your favorite Italian bread with cheese on top, open-faced tuna and tomato sandwiches, even leftover pizza."

Andrew's face was as radiant as the Christmas angel's face on top of the tree.

Before the year of the toaster oven, I'd always been so wrapped up in what the gift was, and whether or not I could use it or if it fit, to pay much attention to the giver. But after poking around in the world's best "art of living" book, I got my head straight about the difference between the gift and the giver.

Now *all* gifts please me... whether they're pink plastic finger hooks or something I have to pick out myself. What's important isn't whether I like it or if it fits my lifestyle. What's important is that by the very act of giving, the giver has demonstrated that he or she loves me, and *that* is the best gift of all.

BRINGING IT TO PASS,
FOOTBALL AND ALL

It was a crisp fall day in Madison, Wisconsin when the University of Wisconsin football team defeated the University of Illinois in our final Big Ten Conference home game of the season. The win guaranteed Wisconsin a chance to play in a postseason Holiday Bowl game for the second year in a row. The previous year Wisconsin had won the Big Ten championship and had gone on to defeat the UCLA Bruins at the Rose Bowl in Pasadena.

Now Wisconsin was headed to the Hall of Fame Bowl in Tampa, Florida over the Christmas holidays. My twenty-two-year-old son Michael, a senior at the University of Wisconsin, was a four-year member of their marching band, famous for their wildly entertaining high-stepping antics that dazzle crowds at every pregame, half-time, and the band's famous "fifth quarter" after each game.

I'd desperately wanted to go to the Rose Bowl game the year before to watch my son perform, but the trip was too expensive. I didn't know anyone in Pasadena to stay with and airfare was out of the question. On New Year's Day 1994 my house was full of relatives as we all watched Michael on TV. He played his drums with such precision during the Rose Bowl parade and game that my heart nearly burst with excitement and pride.

But when the Wisconsin Badgers won the right to play in the Hall of Fame Bowl the very next season, I realized that *that* game would be Michael's last time ever to march with the band before he graduated... my son's last hurrah, so to speak, after four of the most exciting years of his life. I *had* to be there.

Right. A single parent with a small income and bigger-than-life dreams. That's me.

In late November I mentioned my dream to my airline pilot friends who use two of our bedrooms as their Milwaukee-area home away from home. One said he had a couple of low-cost "friend" passes left for the year that fifteen-year-old Andrew and I could use to get to Tampa and back.

"The passes are only about a hundred dollars each, but you'll have to fly standby," he said.

I jumped at the chance as he set things in motion. Next, I had to find housing. I looked on the map and saw that our retired friends, Wally and Shirley, live just forty-five minutes from Tampa. I was sure they'd put us up for the week in their Florida condo.

Everything seemed to be working smoothly until I called my dad in Illinois to tell him the good news. Dad planted my feet back on the ground when he said, "You're going to Florida between Christmas and New Year's? That's the busiest tourist week of the year down there! And you're flying standby? What do you think your chances are of getting on a plane that week?"

My bubble of optimism burst in mid-air once again when I heard on the radio that nearly thirty thousand Wisconsinites had already bought tickets to the Hall of Fame Bowl to see their Badgers play the Duke Blue Devils in Tampa. If you've ever been to Wisconsin in the winter, you can understand why so many people were jumping at the chance to go to a warmer climate for a few days in December and January. Our chances of getting down there flying standby certainly didn't look good. They looked impossible, in fact.

Besides, there was another glitch in the plans. The Milwaukee-based airline we'd be flying on had only one flight a day to Tampa. How could I even think there'd be empty seats on that plane the week between Christmas and New Year's?

I told myself disgustedly, *How could you be so stupid? This will never work!*

In addition to decorating for Christmas, buying gifts, cleaning house, and planning meals for my older children, son-in-law, and granddaughter who would be coming home for Christmas, I now had an additional stressor in my life. How could we possibly get to Florida?

I talked to my friend Heather. Before Heather and her husband, Rusty, moved to Oak Creek the previous summer, Rusty had been one of my houseguest pilots for four months.

"Heather, I already bought four Hall of Fame Bowl tickets so Andrew and I and our friends in Florida can see Michael march in his last game. The tickets cost me $120! And we stand about as much chance of getting on that plane the last week of December as Tampa has of having a two-foot snowfall during the game. What was I thinking?"

Heather smiled and grabbed my hand. "Pat. Stop worrying. Do something for me. Look through the book of Psalms. Read it until you find a verse that seems to be speaking to you."

I looked at Heather as if she'd just told me to go plant a grapefruit tree in my snow-filled backyard.

"Psalms? What am I going to find in there?" I asked Heather.

"Just do it. You'll find what you're looking for."

That afternoon I opened my Bible and read the first two psalms. Nothing hit me. The third verse said something about "bearing luscious fruit each season without fail" which only depressed me more because it made me think of ruby red grapefruit and large juicy oranges hanging on trees all over Florida, fruit that I certainly wouldn't be enjoying.

This can't be the verse that's supposed to make me feel better, I thought. I closed the book and opened it again at random. This time my eyes went directly to Psalms 37:5.

Commit thy way unto the Lord; trust also in Him; and He shall bring it to pass.

Two things about that verse nearly threw me for a loop. The part about committing my way to the Lord... my way to see my son perform in his last game, perhaps? The other was the notion that the Lord would bring it to pass. If I did my part that was God's promise. If I really, truly *trusted* in the Lord, then He would bring it to pass. Also, I have to admit that the word "pass" was a clincher since Andrew and I would be flying standby on a "pass."

OK, Patricia, this is it. If Heather can be so dead-bolt certain of her faith, why can't you? You have to put it on the line. Do you truly believe that this is in the hands of the Lord and that He will bring it to pass?

I only had to ask myself that question once. I sat down that moment and memorized verse 37:5. And if you want to know the truth, it was the first Bible verse I'd ever memorized in my life. I've been a longtime Bible reader and studier, but memorizing is very difficult for me.

But I memorized "Commit thy way unto the Lord; trust also in Him; and He shall bring it to pass." Not only did I memorize it, but I said it at least a hundred times a day during those weeks before Christmas.

The minute I turned the problem over to the Lord, I relaxed completely and virtually sailed through the preparations for Christmas. Never again did I worry about whether or not we'd get on the plane.

One night, one of the pilots staying at my house called the airline's reservations desk and asked for the exact number of tickets that had been sold for those few flights to Tampa during Christmas week. Every flight had been greatly oversold with the exception of Christmas morning. And even for that flight eighty of the eighty-four seats had been sold, with three weeks still to go before Christmas.

Eric shook his head. "I'm sorry, Pat. Wish I could do something to help."

"Well, that's where this trust thing is going to work, Eric," I told my houseguest. "I'm stepping out, ready to march, just like Michael's marching band. I'm trusting in the Lord. We're getting on that plane; I just know it."

Eric smiled and shook his head, no doubt figuring I had a screw loose somewhere. Or perhaps he was just surprised that I'd suddenly become so verbal about my faith.

For the next three weeks I repeated my newly memorized verse a thousand times. Before I got out of bed in the morning, before each meal, during the day, in the car, in my home office, walking down the hall, in bed at night. I repeated it to all my friends and family and assured them that Andrew and I would be in Tampa for the Hall of Fame Bowl on January 2 and that we'd be flying down there on Christmas morning.

Christmas Eve day dawned holy and cold in Milwaukee. My grown children, son-in-law, granddaughter, friends Rusty and Heather and their two little daughters, Andrew, and I all celebrated Christ's birth midst my giggling excitement as I packed our bags for Florida. I shared my memorized Bible verse from Psalms with them as part of the grace before our Christmas Eve dinner.

"So Mom, are you just going to keep going back to the airport every day all week until you get on the plane?" my daughter Julia asked during dessert.

"No, honey, we'll be getting on the plane tomorrow morning. I'll send you postcards and bring you seashells!"

Never before in my life had I been so sure of something, something that to all the sensible people around me seemed to be the folly of the century.

Bags packed, car loaded, Michael drove us to the airport at 7:30 A.M. Christmas Day. The gate agent said there'd been four people with emergencies in Florida, and they'd been given priority standby status. It didn't matter. I knew that when that gate closed we'd be on that plane.

*   *   *

That afternoon Andrew and I picked grapefruit from the tree next to the hot tub in the back yard of our friends' house in Florida, as we celebrated Christmas with new friends and old. Nine days later—after sunning ourselves on Gulf beaches, exploring exotic wonders, and following the Wisconsin marching band as they performed all over Tampa—we watched as the University of Wisconsin defeated Duke in the Hall of Fame Bowl on a beautiful, sunny, eighty-degree day.

Michael's last performance with the band was stellar. But not quite as stellar as my faith in the Lord who brings all things to pass... if we just put our trust in Him.

THE PROMISE OF LIFE

~~~

Right outside our front door is a pointed light fixture, the top of which is only six feet from the concrete porch floor. That spring of 1984 a mother robin chose the top of that light fixture for her nesting place. I quickly came to the conclusion that robins are either the dumbest birds in the world or the most trusting. In spite of the hundreds of daily interruptions caused by the comings and goings of the six of us who used that door almost exclusively, mother and father robin steadfastly built that nest, grass by grass, straw by straw.

Andrew, then four, was totally enthralled by the birds' activity. He was able to witness firsthand the life cycle of mother robin and her family. We kept a hand mirror near the front door during those weeks so we could all make a daily inspection of the inside of the nest. All we had to do was hold the mirror up at arm's length to peer into the birds' sanctuary.

Andrew was enraptured by the big red-breasted bird and her daily routine. We looked up "birds" in the encyclopedia. We talked about how springtime is a time of new birth. We talked about Easter being a time of rebirth.

Before long, four blue eggs appeared in the nest. When any of us approached the door, mother robin took flight from her nest and perched on a nearby maple tree where she could supervise from a distance. Yet, as soon as we were out of sight, she always returned quickly to her egg-warming duties.

One glorious, sun-filled morning Andrew peered into the hand mirror his big sister was holding and squealed, "Mommy, they're out! The birds are out!"

Sure enough, three little gawking, thin-skinned, blue-gray, two-inch-long babies filled the nest. The fourth egg hadn't hatched yet. Now Andrew would be able to see how carefully the mother fed her babies, kept them warm, and protected them. *What a magnificent lesson,* I thought smugly to myself as I answered another barrage of Andrew's "new life" questions.

But the next day, disaster. While mother robin was off hunting worms, the three tiny babies fell out of the nest and landed on the hard concrete below. Andrew and I were on our way into the house after a walk when we spotted the dead birds. I'll never forget the look on my son's face. A sick feeling worked its way from my head to my stomach; I wanted to cry. All that effort building the nest, the mother's time and devotion to her eggs, and now three of her babies were dead. "Why did the other babies die, Mama?" Andrew kept asking. "Why didn't the mom and daddy bird make the nest higher on the sides so the babies couldn't fall out?"

I didn't know what to say to Andrew, who could hardly comprehend such a tragedy. I couldn't stand thinking about it myself. Those birds had become so important to our family.

His questions reminded me of his sadness and confusion a few months earlier when he learned that my sister's first baby had died before it was born. At that time, I had tried to explain to Andrew that Aunt Catherine's baby had some physical problems, and that God had decided to take the tiny little boy into heaven right away, even before he was born.

"Just wait, honey," I continued. "Someday Aunt Catherine and Uncle Bill will have another baby. God almost always gives us a second chance. Remember, that's why Jesus rose from the dead... to give everyone on earth a second chance."

I wanted so much for Andrew to concentrate on the promise of life rather than the mystery of death.

A few days after the birds fell from the nest, the fourth egg hatched, and we all held our breath, hoping he wouldn't fall. But soon the baby bird took flight, precariously, wobbling more than flying. As Andrew and I stood watching from the front porch, the little bird landed clumsily on a nearby bush, then fluttered off to join his mama on a sturdy branch of the budding maple tree.

It wasn't long after that my sister called with news that she and her husband were expecting again. The promise of life was unfolding before us. Andrew, of course, was thrilled.

That night as I paged through my Bible, I came to a verse in Matthew 16:25 and was again reminded of the promise of eternal life in heaven. "Anyone who loses his life for me shall find it again." I read the verse to Andrew, who was still asking questions about my sister's miscarriage and whether or not the new baby would be OK.

After awhile Andrew started talking about the prospect of having a new cousin. He smiled and said, "I don't think this baby will die, Mommy. God doesn't want all the babies early, does he?"

I smiled and in my mind's eye I could still see that last little bird flitting from one branch to another in full protective view of its mother the day it sailed from the nest.

"No, honey, God lets us keep most of them. And when a new baby is born, it's easier to tuck the sadness we felt when the others died deep into our hearts to make room for the joy of the new ones. And you know what, Andrew? God our father is always there, watching out for each one of us... little boys, birds, babies, everyone!"

"Mommy, I think Easter's the best time of all, don't you?"

"Without a doubt, Andrew, without a doubt."

The lessons Andrew and I learned together that spring stayed in our hearts the following year when my husband and I separated. We knew that no matter what, when things go wrong, there is always another opportunity, a second chance, guaranteed by God himself.

Now, THIS Is Happiness

Have you ever asked yourself, "Am I happy?"

Or maybe you think that single parenting by nature includes a certain measure of unhappiness. Most single parents are single because of an event that they did not want or expect: a divorce, the untimely death of a spouse, or an unplanned pregnancy. These things just naturally bring a period of unhappiness.

But at some point, we single parents must accept the fact that we create our own happiness. I discovered long ago that real happiness comes from the smallest things. Beautiful homes, fancy cars, great jobs, and fabulous clothes do not, repeat, DO NOT guarantee happiness. In fact, because of the stress involved in paying for them, they often do just the opposite.

But the little things, ah, now we're talkin'.

For me, the secret to real happiness began quietly, even unconsciously.

It all started when my dad gave me my mother's old steely-blue satin comforter a few years after she died. The moment I felt it, I experienced a clean, crisp exhilaration I had never felt before. At first I couldn't put my finger on the reason for my elation. Was it knowing its cool slippery fineness had touched her cheek the way it does mine? Had she felt the warm comfort of its thick stuffing as she lay down exhausted on the living room sofa for a quick afternoon nap?

Both of my parents appreciated a good nap. My dad was never in a bad mood after his long day as a rural mail carrier because he almost always took a thirty-minute mind-body-and-soul-refreshing afternoon nap. That half-hour of extra sleep gave him the renewed energy to work on other projects late into the day, to play ball or build kites with me in the evening.

So, anyway, there I was, in my forties when Dad presented me with the old blue satin comforter my mother had used for her naps, and suddenly my own afternoon naps took on a whole new meaning. As the single parent of four children, I learned that a half-hour nap under the blue satin comforter, as the late afternoon sun warmed the room, renewed my energy and improved my disposition. That comforter made me happy, a warm, spirit-lifting kind of happiness that I was conscious of every time I slipped under its luxury.

Happiness in its purest form can be found in all kinds of unexpected places. One day at a science store, I picked up two packages of glow-in-the-dark stars. At home that night I enlisted Andrew's help. We brought four dining-room chairs into my bedroom and hopped from chair to chair, from bed to dresser, as we stuck the adhesive-backed stars all over the ceiling. Andrew looked up the constellations in the encyclopedia, and together we created The Bear, Milky Way, Big and Little Dippers, the Great Square, Orion, Pegasus, and Hercules. Then he placed the planets that came with the star kit the right distance from the sun, the center ceiling light.

Andrew and I could hardly wait to close the door and turn off the lights. We fell back on the bed in wonder. The white ceiling looked black, and the stars glittered like diamonds in the night sky. We ooohed and aaahed and pointed out the constellations we'd each created. That was the moment I felt another wave of sheer unabashed happiness. I wondered if God felt the same way when he finished creating the heavens and earth.

Of course we had to create the nighttime sky in Andrew's bedroom the next day. Ever since then we both love to escape under the covers in our bedrooms each night just so we can fall asleep under the stars. Even though it's been years since we put those stars up, I still love that calming feeling of pure happiness when I turn off my light every night.

Soon I discovered my new breadmaker had the same effect

as the comforter and the stars on my spirits. I bought my bread machine after months of deliberation and longing. I consulted *Consumer Reports,* priced different brands, and studied their features. One Sunday, as I glanced through the sale ads, I found my dream machine reduced by almost half. I practically bolted out the door. Within the hour I was a proud owner, and we've been best friends ever since.

Two or three times a week, I toss in the ingredients. When the baking cycle begins, I feel it once again. Pure happiness. It's an aroma infinitely better than perfume or fresh flowers or pine trees. The smell of baking yeast bread stirs my soul and causes me to take lots of deep breaths with eyes closed, basking in aromatic happiness.

Then one day it occurred to me: So far, the things that make me deliciously happy have to do with one of my five senses— the satiny feel of the comforter, the visual cheer of the stars. The breadmaker, of course, tantalized my sense of smell.

Once I caught on to the sensory approach to happiness, I decided to go all the way with it. I wondered if certain tastes and sounds would give me the same unabashed feeling of happiness as the satin comforter, the ceiling stars, and the baking bread.

It didn't take long to discover my "happy tastes and sounds," especially after I posed the question to Andrew.

"Mom, what do you like to taste most in the world?"

I looked at him blankly. Patiently, he tried again.

"What is it that you have forty-five different flavors of on the kitchen counter?"

Of course. My tea. I am a tea fanatic. Here I am old enough to be a grandparent, and I've never had a cup of coffee in my life. But tea, oh my goodness, a huge cup of tea with a little sweetener and a splash of milk, oh, now *that's* happiness. Pure contentment. A passion that speaks of relaxation, calmness, friendship, and warmth.

What sounds make me happy? I wondered. Not necessarily my favorite Beethoven concerto or Mozart, or even the sound of the University of Wisconsin marching band, although that does give me goose bumps. It's not the sound of birds outside my bedroom window on a spring morning, nor the laughter of the neighborhood children as they slide down the hill next to my house on their sleds. No, it's none of those, although they are all music to my ears.

The sounds that stir that old friend "happiness" within me are these:

It's Jeanne, my oldest daughter, calling me from her California college to exclaim, "Mom, I made the Dean's list!"

It's Julia, my second oldest, calling from the hospital, "Mom, she's a beautiful, healthy girl, and we named her Hailey!"

It's Michael, my oldest son, calling me from Madison, "Mom, we're going to the Rose Bowl! The whole band! I'll be playing in Pasadena at the Rose Bowl game!"

It's Andrew, still in high school, saying "I love you!" as he dashes out the door to catch the school bus every morning.

It's my daughter-in-law, Amy, squeezing me in a bear hug, saying, "You're the greatest!"

Yes, it's all of these intangible expressions of excitement and love from my children, the people I treasure most in the world, that make me deliriously happy.

Today, why don't you make a list of the things that make you truly happy? If nothing comes to mind, make plans to watch the sunrise some morning. Or find ten people to hug tomorrow. Bake something from scratch. Wear something really, truly comfortable to work.

Happiness. It's out there. You just have to think about it. Sometimes all it takes is appreciating the smallest things you can imagine.

NIFTY FIFTY

~~~

"Come on, Mom, I'm really hungry for a big cheeseburger and fries. Can't we go out to eat?" Andrew implored.

"No. Fast food is too expensive. We've got meatloaf at home," I snapped.

As my fiftieth birthday loomed just over the horizon, I'd become a money-hoarding crab.

I'd loved my forties. They were fun, energetic, and full of life. I'd accomplished a lot during my forties. A month before I turned forty, I became a single parent to my four children, but thanks to team effort and lots of prayer, we survived the next decade beautifully. I not only got the three oldest through their teenage years without my acquiring too many new gray hairs, they were now college graduates living on their own and supporting themselves with interesting careers. I just had the youngest, Andrew, still at home... a terrific high-school sophomore involved in sports and band.

Yes, indeed, my forties had been happy years, filled with meaning and purpose. But I just wasn't sure about turning fifty, and the big day in October was just months away. That July things started to go downhill.

The day before I was to leave on vacation, I received a notice from the Social Security office. I tore open the letter. "You are no longer eligible for benefits..."

"I don't understand this," I blubbered to the representative on the phone.

She responded kindly. "If a minor child only has one living parent, that parent receives financial help from Social Security until the child is sixteen. The child continues to receive it until he's eighteen, however."

I hung up the phone in a daze. In four months one-third of my annual income would be gone.

Well, it was too late to cancel the vacation. My daughter in California was eagerly awaiting our arrival. And besides, I'd saved like the dickens for six months to pay for the trip. So, instead of worrying about the future, I repeated my favorite Bible verse over and over.

Commit thy way unto the Lord; trust also in Him; and He shall bring it to pass. **Psalms 37:5**

The day we arrived in Oakland, a huge portion of my back tooth broke into little pieces. Three weeks later, when we returned home and the crown was put in, I had to shell out $487 to my dentist. I had no dental insurance, of course.

The next day I received a bill for x-rays of my arthritic toe... $144. The meager medical insurance I could afford didn't cover x-rays.

That same week I noticed I was having trouble reading the fine print and sometimes even the medium print. Out of desperation I purchased a huge light for the kitchen that contained four four-foot-long fluorescent bulbs. It made cooking, bill paying, reading, and letter writing at the kitchen counter much easier for my "approaching fifty" eyes. But that new light set me back $107.

Next, I made a trip to the optometrist's office. He said both my distance and close-up vision were worse. That office visit, including the bill for the new distance and reading glasses, was $241.

That same week, I finally gave in to one too many backaches caused by my ancient desk chair. I figured that the lower back pain was just another pitfall of approaching the big FIVE-OH.

But once again, I repeated my favorite verse from Psalms, stepped out in faith, and wrote out a check for $105 for a superb office chair with arms and lumbar support. The week after I put that chair together, I noticed a great improvement in my back.

Well, now, at least my broken tooth was fixed, I could see near and far with my new glasses, my back didn't hurt, and my arthritic toe felt lots better. Things seemed to be looking up.

Then I sat down at my computer and started adding.

```
Crown for tooth: . . . . . . . . . . . . . . .$487
X-rays for toe:  . . . . . . . . . . . . . . . .144
Kitchen light:  . . . . . . . . . . . . . . . . .107
Bifocals & reading glasses:  . . . . . . . .241
Desk chair for back pain: . . . . . . . . . .105
Total:  . . . . . . . . . . . . . . . . . . . . .$1084
```

I took a deep breath and, once again, committed it all to the Lord. I was simply too busy to worry about it.

The next day I discovered that while we were in California lightning had struck our TV set, destroying the picture and the sound. I can easily do without a TV, but Andrew often brings his friends to our family room to watch movies, and the airline pilots who stay with us like to relax in front of the TV, especially when they're on reserve. So that week I wrote out another check for a good second-hand TV... $250.

Things were getting out of hand. First my income was going down by a third, then all those unexpected bills. I wasn't just going "over the hill" age-wise, I was careening out of control, financially as well as physically.

And so I prayed. "Lord, please give my guardian angel a nudge. I need a little help down here. Thank you, Lord, for providing for my son and me." Of course I ended the prayer with the verse from Psalms.

A few days later while I was still wallowing in self-pity over my pending birthday, I received a letter from a publisher. As I opened the letter, a check tumbled out. The year before I'd written a few short daily devotionals for their annual book, but I'd already been paid for my work the previous spring.

The letter explained that in honor of their twentieth year of publication, they'd turned the distribution of the book over to a larger publisher who expected sales to skyrocket. The original publisher was sharing the advance on the royalties with all the writers of the book. My share was $1,338.

All I could do was nod skyward toward my guardian angel with a banana-sized grin. Then I grabbed my calculator. But even before I added the cost of the TV to my list of five "getting older" expenses, I knew that the check I was holding would cover it all.

The bills totaled $1,334. That guardian angel of mine, the one with the math background, gave me enough money for all those expenses plus two big juicy cheeseburgers and fries.

That night as Andrew and I chowed down at his favorite fast food place, I said what I'd been thinking all day.

"Andrew, turning fifty isn't so bad. I think my fifties are going to be my best decade yet. My guardian angel and the Lord will see to it."

OPEN YOUR HEART TO CHANGE

One thing we single parents need to know is that it's never too late for love. It may not happen this year or next. Of course, you may never find the perfect spouse and that's OK. You'll probably discover, as I have, that the longer you live your life as a single person, the more you like it, or at least the more comfortable you become with it.

Many single parents don't find the perfect "other" until their children are grown, and they're well into middle or advanced age.

I know a woman whose father, a widower, recently remarried. That woman was dead set against the marriage, and now finds that her "stepmother" is "absolutely awful! "She makes me feel like an outsider in my father's house! She wants my father all to herself and even had the nerve to get rid of Mother's furniture and linens!"

Every time I saw this woman, she had more and more complaints about her stepmother. One time she was upset that they were spending two or three months every winter in Florida.

Funny thing, though: whenever I saw her dad and stepmom, they seemed to be deliriously happy. The daughter is the only one who's miserable. And she's wallowing in it, making it worse every year.

Now let me tell you about my own father, Ed Kobbeman. Same thing happened to him.

In 1979, after thirty-five years of happy marriage, my mother died at age fifty-seven.

Three years later, Dad remarried a cute blonde Norwegian named Bev. I'd only been with Bev a couple of times before the wedding, but each time I could tell how happy she and Dad were together.

Oh, there were times when I wondered how it would feel to have another woman living in the house my dad built in 1947, the house we children grew up in and that my mother had lovingly decorated all the years we were living at home. How would it be to have another woman in Mother's home?

Well, even though I loved my mother deeply, I honestly believe an angel was sitting on Dad's shoulder when he met, dated, and married Bev. Without a doubt, she is a gem, a beautiful human being whose optimistic personality, ready-to-do-anything-or-go-anywhere attitude adds sparkle to Dad's life.

Over the years they've redecorated nearly every room in the house and, thanks to Bev's beautiful taste, the home of my childhood is lovelier today than it was when I was growing up.

Three months after they were married, Dad had a heart attack. Bev lovingly nursed him back to health and encouraged him to go walking or biking with her every day. They've been married since 1982; now in their seventies, they still go dancing many Saturday nights, travel the world, and entertain their many friends and relatives.

I don't even like to think what life would have been like for my dad all these years if he'd never met Bev. I honestly believe he'd be a sad, lonely, old man. Instead, because he moved his life forward with a new woman and a new love, he's vibrant, healthy, and as delightful and interesting as he is happy.

I'm glad that the good Lord gave me the courage to tuck the warm, wonderful memories I have of my own mother into the back of my heart and to allow the good, new feelings I have for my stepmother to blossom and flourish. It seems that if we just open our hearts and minds to change, life just gets better and better as we get older. I know one thing: it certainly has for my dad, thanks to Bev.

AT THE EDGE OF THE CONTINENT

Ever since I became a single parent, I had nightmares about how I would put my three teenagers through college at once. But when it was time for Jeanne, my oldest, to go, amazingly, everything fell neatly into place.

I'd filled out all the college financial-aid forms for grants and loans. Jeanne's art slides impressed judges, who awarded her a half-tuition scholarship to our hometown University of Wisconsin at Milwaukee. The United States government came through with a grant for the rest of her tuition. At first we wondered how she would have enough for living expenses, but then a friend at work told me about a woman near campus who was looking for a college student to live in her home.

Lottie was a warm, sensitive art lover who would appreciate Jeanne's talents. Herself a single parent, Lottie simply needed someone to stay with her eleven-year-old daughter four nights a week while she worked. For this small responsibility Jeanne would receive free room and board for the year.

"Jeanne, do you realize that, except for the cost of your books, your whole first year of college is costing us nothing?"

"I know, Mom. And if I get a part-time job, I can start saving for next year so I can transfer to a really great art school somewhere out of state."

I couldn't think about my daughter moving far away again. She'd just returned from her year studying art in Yugoslavia as a foreign exchange student, thanks to the scholarship she'd won. Now that she was starting college, I was delighted that Jeanne would be living only twenty minutes away.

School began and everything was perfect. For the first time in over a year I could call my daughter whenever I liked and it wouldn't cost a penny, compared to the outrageous phone bills I'd had the previous year when I phoned her a few times in Yugoslavia. Jeanne must have felt the phone freedom too, because when school started she called me nearly every day to gab about her classes, her teachers, and about the funny antics of the eleven-year-old in her charge.

The first weekend Jeanne came home to Oak Creek on the city bus so we could "hang out together," as she called it. She played with her little brother, did her laundry, and baked cookies. All weekend we gabbed, shared secrets, and hugged each other often. We'd become two adult friends who truly cherished one another.

The next Friday, two weeks after school began, my daughter Julia called me at work.

"She did what?" I yelled into the phone as I felt my cheeks become hot and my eyes fill with tears.

"Mom, Jeanne's gone! She left Lottie a note saying she was sorry, but that she had a chance to go to California with her friend, Greg."

"She just left without saying good-bye? She didn't even leave us a note?" I stammered, barely able to talk.

"There's nothing here, Mom."

I felt like I had just fallen out of an airplane and was spinning hopelessly out of control. *How could she be so selfish?* I thought. *How could she do this after I worked so hard to get her that scholarship, the grant, and the free room and board? How could she throw a free year of college down the drain? How could she just up and leave without saying good-bye?*

Gone with Jeanne were my dreams of sharing a wonderful year with my oldest daughter. None of my children had ever made such a terrible mistake.

Four days later a letter arrived.

Dear Mom,

    I know I've hurt you, and although it may take some time I hope you will eventually understand my reasons and forgive me. I am not going to California to get married, become pregnant, do drugs, act lazy, join a cult, or escape from my family. I'm going West to improve my life, to learn and explore and to seek new opportunities. I know my way will be hard and that is the way I prefer. I am not leaving you behind, because I love you very much. The only thing I regret about leaving is not being able to say goodbye. When I decided to do this I realized that I wouldn't be able to discuss this with you in a rational way.

Well, she was right about that last part, at least. And the three-page typewritten letter I sent stating exactly what I thought of her sense of adventure made that plain.

In the meantime, in Palo Alto, Jeanne was hired by another single parent who needed live-in help. She cleaned house, did the cooking, and took care of the woman's eight-year-old daughter in the afternoons.

Still furious, I sarcastically told her in another letter that I hoped she was enjoying her "June Cleaver" life of cooking, cleaning, and child care. How could my bright, talented child throw away a free education for this?

Jeanne's second letter arrived two weeks later.

Dear Mom,

    Today was my first day working at a bookstore, if you can call it that. The enjoyment and knowledge I'm getting out of it hardly makes it work. Jerry, the store's owner, is sensitive and intelligent. He paints and will be quite a resource as far as the cultural scene here goes. All around me are possibilities!

    I spent last weekend camping on an obscure beach with Rebecca, my friend from Milwaukee. When we awoke, several seals were feeding near the shore. They followed us down as we combed the beach for amazing things left by the sea. Neither of us could believe that we are on the very edge of the continent. I love you, Jeanne.

Jeanne continued to work at the bookstore and became close friends with the owner and his wife. Jeanne also drove a two ton truck and picked up recyclables during her other part-time job at the Stanford University Recycling Center.

A few months later, when we talked on the phone, Jeanne admitted to me that she and her friend Greg, had actually lived in his small car for a month before they moved into an octagon-shaped house in the mountains with four friends. I was horrified. She thought it a great adventure; "character-building," she called it.

Right after they moved into the house in the mountains, she wrote to tell me that the electric company did not have a grid out to their house. What little electricity they had was supplied by a noisy gas-powered generator they cranked on each evening to give them enough light to read by and enough power to keep the refrigerator cold.

I thought it sounded primitive. Jeanne thought it was like Laura Ingalls Wilder from *Little House on the Prairie*. And environmentally correct, to boot.

The following year Jeanne found a job working for a print-maker at a gallery in downtown San Francisco. He taught her the art of printmaking, a job that helped pay for her freshman year of classes at Foothill Junior College.

"Straight A's, Mom, can you believe it?" she wrote. "I never got straight A's in my life!"

After a year at the junior college, Jeanne moved to another group house in Oakland (an old Victorian... *with* electricity) and enrolled in a four-year fine arts college, the California College of Arts and Crafts, where she graduated with honors and a four-year fine arts degree in 1994.

During the years after Jeanne left abruptly for California, she taught me what a true education is really all about.

The year before, when she was in Yugoslavia living with a Communist family, I worried that she was on the "edge of the continent," ready to fall off into a sea of political confusion, uncertainty, and inexperience. When she returned home, I pulled her back into safe territory, close to me, with the lure of a scholarship, a grant, and a comfortable place to live near our convenient, safe, hometown university.

But Jeanne had a different plan. And hers was not the safe, conservative option. Her plan was to redefine the meaning of a "true" education. Jeanne learned about seals by sleeping near them on the beach. She learned about art by working for artists. She learned about finances by claiming independence and filling out her own scholarship, grant, and loan applications. She learned about life by tasting every mouthful, one morsel at a time.

In the meantime, I, too, am becoming educated... for this mother has learned the hard way that letting go means letting her go *her* way, not mine. I've also learned that the education she received *her* way will take her far in life... much further, indeed, than the edge of the continent.

PART THREE:

~~~

FRIENDSHIP MATTERS

DANCING LESSONS

I'd been a single parent for five years. Five years of being a fortysomething mother of four, with a job and a six-bedroom house to maintain.

I worried about everything. About whether the sump pump would conk out during a big rain and flood my family room when I wasn't home. I worried about wasp's nests in the overhang and about broken tree limbs. I worried about how, on my meager income, I would put three teenagers through college at the same time.

I also worried about how I would ever find a nice man to date. And about how sad it would be to grow old alone when all my children were gone.

Some Saturday nights I made lists of the qualities I wanted in a man. He had to be close to my age, intelligent, have a great sense of humor, a lover of children, faith-filled, non-smoker, athletic, good-looking, tall, a handyman, considerate, easygoing, financially secure.... Funny thing, though, that guy has never been on my doorstep when the doorbell rang.

I also prayed. Yes, I prayed every night for Mr. Perfect to come along. After months went by and I still didn't meet anyone, I prayed harder and shortened my list of qualities: "OK, Lord, how about a nice man with deep faith and a great sense of humor." I expected God to just sort of plop this man into my life.

One day the phone rang. It was a very nice man with a deep voice telling me I'd won a free dance lesson.

"It only lasts an hour, and you'll learn lots of different dance steps."

As soon as I hung up the phone, I could feel my face flush. *Go to a dance? A real party? Me? What if I step on my instructor's toes and make a fool of myself?* I anguished.

When I arrived at the class the following week, I was bombarded with "nice" people. I mean, *really* nice. Oh, so very nice. Bordering on gag-me-with-a-spoon nice.

"Hello there! My, that's a lovely coat."

I was wearing an old dark gray wool jacket that my daughter had worn in high school. It was about as "lovely" as my scuffed black flats.

After the introductions, a woman elegantly dressed in a black chiffon skirt and silver spangled high-heeled shoes glided toward me, followed by two twentysomething young men. She reached for my hand. "Hello, there, Ms. Lorenz. I'm Ms. Leopold, one of the instructors. This is Mr. Bates. And here's Mr. Ross. We only use last names here. We like to keep it formal. Ballroom dancing, you know, is very serious."

Serious? I wondered. These were not serious people.

With giant grins etched onto their faces and their happy feet tip-tapping around the dance floor, they were bouncy, peppy, light-on-their-feet little gremlins. Definitely not *serious*. This was happy feet land. I wasn't sure I was ready for all this happiness.

"All right now," one of the instructors called out cheerily, "everyone join hands and make a big circle. We're going to learn to do the 'push-pull.' Pretend you're squishing grapes. Right foot back, ladies, and squish! Now left foot forward and squish! Now pretend you're marching in a parade. Right foot forward and flat on the floor, march! Left foot down, march! So it's squish, squish, march, march."

I did it with the others. Squished my grapes, marched my parade. Squish, squish, march, march. Over and over.

Then we had to do it with a partner. Oh, what a delicious addition to the "hey we're having a happy time here aren't we" mood, when Mr. Ross, one of the most handsome of the half-my-age instructors, rushed over to take my hand.

I felt my heart beating a little faster as Mr. Ross and I squish-squished and march-marched for a few minutes as I repeated the words over and over to myself with each beat of the music.

But then something awful happened. Mr. Ross started asking me questions… while we were push-pulling!

"So how do you like dancing? And what do you do for a living?"

Two questions, and here I was trying desperately to keep my squish-squish, march-march in order. I could just feel what was about to happen. The minute I opened my mouth to answer, my squishes and marches got crossed. The smile never left his face when I stepped on his toes. "It's OK, Ms. Lorenz. That's why we're here. We're going to teach you how to do all this automatically, without thinking. We're going to teach you how to look good on the dance floor even if you're dancing with a bad dancer. You'll learn all the basic dances: fox trot, waltz, rumba, jitterbug, mambo, cha-cha…."

All that in thirty-five minutes? I wondered as I glanced at the large wall clock.

"Are you sure you've never had dance lessons before?" questioned the handsome one. "You're so light on your feet!"

Squish-squish. "No, never did." *March-march.*

"So, what do you do?"

"I," *squish-squish*, "I'm a copywriter for a radio" *march-march* "station." *Squish-squish* "… write radio commercials." *March-march.*

"And what do you do for fun? Are you married? Do you go dancing very often?"

All this from a man who refuses to tell me his first name? I thought helplessly.

"Well, I don't do" *squish-squish* much dancing socially, not married," *march-march*, "haven't danced for years, kinda rusty." *March-squish.* "Whoops… sorry about that. By the way, my name's Pat."

Mr. Ballerina didn't flinch. I wondered if torture would get him to tell me his first name.

Finally, when the music ended, the instructors walked each guest, arm-in-arm, across the floor to a couple of "guest" tables set up along the side of the floor. It was time to watch the instructors put on a demonstration.

Poetry in motion. Straight out of the thirties. Arms 'a flying. Legs reaching for the sky. I could just see myself on the dance floor at my cousin's wedding... my heel up on my prince's shoulder for that split second while he twirled me so fast my full chiffon skirt would brush my cheek romantically before we ended our dance with his strong hands on my hips as he lifted me high above his head in a stunning spin finish. For a few fleeting seconds I was Ginger Rogers. Then suddenly Mr. Ross and the Happy Feet Gang descended upon my table.

"Just sign here, Ms. Lorenz. One complete hour-long lesson with your very own private dance instructor, a $65 value, for just $5."

"What?" Another lesson before I really learn anything? I sat back in my chair and shot Mr. Happy Feet a look that would have put a SCUD missile into orbit.

I wasn't happy about having to come back to Happy Feet Land. I knew the going rate for beginners *after* the $5 class was about $40 an hour and up. No way could I afford to fork out big bucks for dance lessons. And I wasn't looking forward to what I knew would be the "hard sell" during that $5 lesson. But for a full hour lesson, the price was certainly right... and just maybe, I thought, God will allow my prince, Mr. Perfect, to show up that night.

At home I wondered, *Is this dancing experience really how God plans to send me the man of my dreams?* I was a small-town girl, raised on sixties rock and roll. Ballroom dancing scared me.

Official dance lesson day arrived. Of course I'd been praying daily that I'd meet an older dance instructor or another student who would "sweep me off my feet" and end my life of lonely Saturday nights.

Mr. Bates, one of the instructors who looked like he hadn't yet had his fifth high-school reunion, stood before me and reached for my hand as if it were a paper-thin porcelain teacup. He carefully placed my hand upon his forearm as we glided ever-so-lightly onto the dance floor.

Then we waltzed. Fox-trotted. Rumba'd. He kept talking, asking me more and more personal questions while I tried desperately to keep my unhappy feet responding gracefully to his happy ones. More questions. I wondered if he was writing a book about my life. But mostly I was just trying to squish-squish, not step on his feet, answer his questions, and figure out if his smile muscles ever ached.

After forty-five minutes of squish-squish, march-march, question-question, talk about me, but not about him... Mr. Bates ushered me into "The Room." I knew the minute he closed the door and the four dark big-flowered-print wall-papered walls started to squeeze in on me that this was the place where they really tried to force you to sign on the dotted line. What dotted line? The dotted line just under the part that said, "Ten one-hour lessons for $550, plus a $150 discount because you're such a swell, happy, light-on-your-feet person."

Mr. Bates started talking about my life, my social habits, my children, my lack of exercise, my need for more friends, my cash flow, the trouble I had meeting "nice" men, my career, my lonely Saturday nights, and my personal habits. (He'd taken good notes during our squish-squish, question-question routine in class.)

He talked and smiled. He flattered me. He made taking dancing lessons a synonym for turning my not-so-social life into a blaze of filled dance cards and stand-in-line gentlemen callers.

Hoping to divert his attention and change the focus of this

humiliating inquisition, I asked him why he'd gotten his master's in urban economics and was now a full-time dance instructor. As soon as the words were out of my mouth, Mr. Happy got happier. Every sentence he sputtered ended with an exclamation point.

"It's fun! Life is supposed to be fun! Dancing is fun! It's great exercise! It's a wonderful way to be with people! It's...." He went for ten straight minutes, and I started to hate urban economics.

At last he took a breath and touched my hand as he gently slid the contract under my fingers, still smiling that happy smile. His eyes sparkled. I felt his happy feet tapping under the desk.

I reached for the pen. On four lines of the contract I wrote very slowly in neat, happy letters:

No money.
Ain't funny.
Too bad.
So sad.

I stood up, smiled my last happy smile, grabbed my coat, and bounded up the stairs toward the light.

A few weeks later I called some old friends and invited them to join me for a night on the town. After dinner we visited an old-fashioned sixties rock-and-roll club. We rocked, we rolled, we boogied, we did The Twist. We laughed until our sides ached and danced until our legs gave out.

The thing I learned from those dance lessons is that it's up to me to make my life fun. Instead of waiting for Mr. Perfect, I have to pick up the phone and make plans with my friends. Having a social life depends on me. Sitting home feeling sorry for myself just doesn't cut it.

Whether you're twenty-five, forty-five, or seventy-five, in order to have friends, you must *be* a friend first. You have to make the first phone call and get things organized. Even if it means taking dancing lessons!

THE HUMBUG HOLIDAYS
AND THE LEAN-TO SNOWMAN

~~~

I was going through the motions. Everything a good mom is supposed to do before Christmas. Lugged out the boxes of holiday decorations. Baked my every-year-the-same-two-kinds-of-cookies. Even bought a real Christmas tree for a change. I remembered how my teenagers grumbled at the wimpy, hand-me-down plastic tree Dad had given us the year before.

I was going through the motions, but my heart was bogged down with a dull ache. I wasn't looking forward to Christmas one bit. My divorce had been finalized the past April, and my husband was already remarried. My oldest daughter, Jeanne, was in Yugoslavia and wouldn't be home for the holidays, the first time ever that all four of my children wouldn't be with me for Christmas. Plus the annual New Year's Eve family get-together weekend at my folks' house with my sister and brother and their families had been cancelled, so I didn't even have the trip to Illinois to look forward to.

I was tired and grumpy. My job writing radio commercials at Milwaukee's biggest radio station was getting more hectic every day. It seemed like every store in town wanted to advertise on the radio during the holiday season, and that meant longer and longer hours at work for me and less time at home with the children.

Then there was the real nemesis, holiday shopping, a chore I kept putting off even though the holiday celebrations were almost here. I had to plan my annual holiday party for the neighbors, Andrew's eighth birthday December 27, and Julia's seventeenth birthday on January 4. How would I get through it all when "bah humbug" was on the tip of my tongue every day?

During the night of December 15, a snowstorm ripped through Wisconsin, dumping twelve inches of snow upon us. Even though Milwaukee is usually prepared for the worst, this blizzard finished its onslaught just before rush hour traffic, bringing the interstate highways to a standstill. The next day all the schools and most businesses were closed. Even the radio station where I worked, eighteen miles from my home, was urging early-morning risers to stay in bed because the roads were definitely not passable.

Fifteen-year-old Michael started making blueberry pancakes for everybody. Julia did a few cheerleading jumps in the living room then invited her neighborhood friends over to watch a movie.

After viewing the picture-postcard scene in our yard and filling up on Michael's splendid flapjacks, I grabbed Andrew and, forgetting my down-in-the-dumps attitude, said, "Come on, buddy, let's make a snowman."

Andrew and I scooped up big handfuls of the wet, perfect-packing snow and built a base fit for a kingpin. Andrew rolled a ball of snow for the next level into such a huge mass that I had to get down on my hands and knees to shove it toward our mighty base with my "shoulder to the wheel."

When I hoisted Andrew's third boulder onto this Amazon snowperson, I felt like Wonder Woman pressing a hundred pounds.

"Andrew, we have to stop this! I can't reach any higher!"

"Mom, we have to make a head. I'll make the head smaller."

As our Wilt-the-Stilt snowman reached a solid seven feet tall, I carefully placed Andrew's bowling-ball-sized snow head on top with the help of a stool I brought out from the house.

"Now the face, Mom. He needs a great face." While I smoothed the snow and pounded arms and a waistline into our giant snowman, Andrew ran inside to get one of his favorite hats from his hat collection.

Andrew returned with a silly beach hat with built-in sunglasses for eyes. "Great hat, huh, Mom? And here's my Superman cape. The 'S' stands for 'Super Snowman'. Let's put it on his front."

I stuck a carrot under the hat for "Super Snowman's" nose and wrapped a long black strap around his middle for a belt.

Andrew and I stepped back to admire our noble snowman. Straight and tall. Ruler of the front yard. When I took their picture, Andrew's head barely reached the snowman's middle.

It was warmer the next morning, and when I looked outside the kitchen window I noticed that Super Snowman seemed to be leaning forward a little. I hoped he wouldn't fall over before Andrew got home from school that day.

Late that afternoon when I returned home after a hectic, make-up-all-the-work-from-yesterday day at the radio station, I saw that our snowman hadn't fallen over, but he was leaning even farther forward at a very precarious forty-five-degree angle. His posture reminded me of the way I felt. Tired, crabby, out-of-sorts, and with the weight of the world on my shoulders.

The next morning Super Snowman was leaning so far forward that I was sure it was a physical impossibility. I had to walk out into the yard to see him up close. *What on earth is holding him up?* I wondered, absolutely amazed.

The Superman cape, instead of being plastered to his front, now dangled freely in the wind as old Frosty's bent chest, shoulders, and head were almost parallel to the ground.

My own shoulders sagged beneath the weight of depression as I remembered that Christmas was almost here. A letter from Jeanne arrived saying that the family she was living with in Yugoslavia didn't celebrate Christmas and, since it wasn't a national holiday, she'd have to go to school on December 25. I missed Jeanne's smile, her wacky sense of humor, and her contagious holiday spirit. I was miserable not having her home during the holidays.

Then I looked out on the patio and saw that my "real" Christmas tree, the one I'd propped up outside to keep fresh until the week before Christmas, had fallen over, smashing some of its branches. "What else is going to go wrong this year?" I wailed out loud, though no one was around to hear me.

The fourth day after we built the snowman was Saturday, the 19th, the day I'd promised to take Andrew to Chicago on the train. Andrew loved the adventure of his first train and taxi rides, the trip to the top of the world's tallest building, the visit to the Shedd Aquarium, and the toy departments of every major store on State Street. But I was depressed by the fact that it rained all day, that the visibility at the top of the Sears Tower was zero, and that the all-day adventure left me totally exhausted.

Late that night after the two-hour train ride back to Milwaukee, Andrew and I arrived home, only to be greeted by the snowman, who by this time, after a warmer day of drizzling rain, was now totally bent over from its base and perfectly parallel to the ground... and yet still balanced six inches above the slushy snow.

That's me out there, I said to myself. *About to fall face down into a snowbank.* But why didn't our snowman fall? Nothing, absolutely nothing, was supporting the weight of that seven-foot-tall giant.

Just like there isn't anything or anybody supporting me during this awful holiday season, I blubbered mentally.

I thought back to the previous days and wondered again what it was that had supported the snowman in such a precarious position. Was it God in his almighty power? A freak of nature? Or a combination of ice, wind, rain, and snow that had bonded to the mighty Super Snowman? Whatever it was, I had a feeling there was a lesson to be learned from watching his decline. The lesson came to me gradually during the next two weeks.

On Christmas Eve, at the children's insistence, I was comforted by our tradition of attending the family Christmas Eve Mass at our parish church. And even though they're not crazy about oysters, the kids insisted I make the traditional German oyster stew supper afterwards. That reminded me of all the wonderful Christmases I'd had at home in Illinois as a child.

Then Andrew brought out his children's Bible for the yearly reading of the Christmas story before the children and I opened the gifts we were exchanging.

Later that night my dear friends Bob and Betsy and their children joined us for Christmas punch and cookies, and then insisted that we join them at the midnight candlelight service at their church.

At 1:00 A.M. when we returned home, I called Jeanne. It was 8 o'clock Christmas morning in Yugoslavia, and Jeanne told me excitedly about the wonderful midnight Mass some friends from school had taken her to, and how she'd heard all her favorite traditional hymns sung in Croatian. She said her "mom" was taking the day off work to cook her a fabulous Yugoslavian feast.

The next day Bob and Betsy offered to be the co-host and hostess for my big neighborhood party. With their help, the event, complete with a talent show, went off without a hitch amidst the mirth and merriment of twenty-five neighbors, who all pitched in with food and beverages.

On December 27, Andrew was delighted with his three-person birthday party. Afterwards, I took the boys to a Walt Disney movie. And the next weekend my out-of-town family decided to get together for a long New Year's Eve weekend at *my* house, filling our home with the madcap merriment of ten houseguests.

And when Julia simplified another dilemma by saying that all she wanted for her birthday was a watch and "lunch out with Mom," I smiled all day.

All in all the holidays, birthdays, and parties that permeated the Lorenz household during the season were joyful, fun-filled, and hardly depressing, thanks to the help and support of so many friends, relatives, and neighbors.

I learned that no matter how depressed, overwhelmed, saddened, lonely, or stressed-out we get, there's always someone or something to help us find or recapture our own inner strength, just like there was for the falling-down, stoop-shouldered Super Snowman, who, during his four-day lifespan, showed me an amazing strength within.

CRASH PAD
❧❧

When I answered the phone that day in March of 1994, I had no idea that my life and my lifestyle were about to change. It was my friend and neighbor, Bruce Swezey, who lives with his wife, Tracey, just two blocks from Andrew and me. Bruce is a part-time pilot for the Air National Guard and had just been hired as a full-time pilot for Midwest Express Airlines, based in Milwaukee.

"So Bruce, how's ground school going?"

"That's why I'm calling, Pat. It's terrific, but I have a favor to ask. There are twelve guys in my class from all over the country. Most of them are living in flea-bag hotels to save money while they're in ground school. You've got some extra bedrooms now that your older kids are out on their own. Why don't you and Andrew take in a couple of guys during our ground school, for a month or so?"

"Houseguests for that long? Would I have to cook for them?" Bruce's idea didn't sound like much fun.

"No. Tracey and I put two guys in our extra room in the basement. They've got a microwave and small refrigerator down there. We don't even see them unless we get together to study. You could make a little money, and they'd have a nicer place to stay. They're great guys, Pat. One just retired from the Air Force. Another was a Navy pilot. They're married and have kids, and I know they'd be happier in a home environment."

"Well, let me think about it, Bruce. I'll talk to Andrew. Strangers in our home for that long might make him feel uncomfortable."

"No problem, Pat, call me when you decide."

It was true that Andrew, who was fourteen at the time, and I were sort of banging around in our big house ever since the three older kids left. I'd turned one bedroom into an office when I quit my job to start working out of my home. Another bedroom became a combination sewing room for me and guest room for my friends and relatives who popped in. But there were two bedrooms and a full bath downstairs that we didn't use at all.

"So Andrew, what do you think about Bruce's idea?" I asked after explaining the details to him.

"Fine with me. Will I still get to watch TV in the family room downstairs when I want?"

"Sure. Sometimes we might need to stay upstairs in the living room if the pilots need to study, but I doubt if they'll disturb your life much."

Secretly I was thinking it would be good for Andrew to have other people around so he could learn to share space and time and the things in our home with other people. The way it was, he had the run of the place and didn't have to share a thing with anyone.

I'd also worried about how a single mom can possibly teach her son how to be a man. My dad, brother, brother-in-law, and uncles all lived out of state; we didn't see them often enough for them to have much impact as role models for Andrew. Even Andrew's older brother, Michael, eight years his senior, was two hours away, finishing his last two years at the University of Wisconsin. With Michael's two part-time jobs and his full-time class schedule, he rarely made it home except for holidays.

Even though the pilots would be good company for Andrew, I still wasn't sure about the idea of having two or three men move in downstairs. How would I feel about my loss of privacy? Would they talk too much and interrupt my writing time? Would they be noisy? Sloppy? Who would clean their bathroom? Me? Not on your life.

Questions and more questions. If they wanted to do their own cooking, where would they keep their food? I'd have to give up space in my cupboards. Would I have to make their beds after I washed their sheets? What about the phone? Would they be making long-distance calls on my bill?

I called my brother Joe in Louisville who is a pilot for UPS. Joe owns two houses, "crash pads" as they're called in the industry, that he rents out to sixteen other pilots who are based in Louisville but live elsewhere.

Joe thought the idea of opening up my own "crash pad" in my home sounded like a good one.

"Pilots are great guys," Joe said with a chuckle. "We're all college degreed, intelligent, interesting characters. You'll be OK. Just put some rules on paper and tell 'em up front what you expect."

I typed up my list of "Crash Pad Do's and Don'ts" including the fact that they'd have to do their own cooking, but they could use my kitchen supplies, pots, pans, dishes, and spices. I'd give them their own cupboard for groceries and a shelf in the refrigerator. I'd wash sheets and towels for them but they'd have to remake their own beds and clean the downstairs bathroom. I'd want them to make a donation to the "Crash Pad" fund, enough to pay the extra utilities and hopefully a portion of the house taxes for the month.

I prayed about the decision, talked to Andrew again, and finally called Bruce a few days later.

"OK, Bruce, send over a couple of the pilots. If they like the place, they can stay here. I figure I can survive anything for thirty days."

The next day Wade and Ron moved in. A couple weeks later Lyle joined them. One of my extra rooms had twin beds so that worked fine.

Wade was a retired Air Force pilot whose family lived in Colorado Springs. He'd been one of General Norman Schwarzkopf's personal pilots during Desert Storm and had all sorts of interesting tales to share with Andrew and me during those early evenings when we were all cooking and gabbing and laughing in the kitchen while we fixed our dinners.

Ron was the Navy pilot whose family lived in Dallas. He'd flown "Top Gun" type planes as well as helicopters during his career and was also a well of information for Andrew as we pumped him with questions about military life.

When Lyle moved in, a vegetarian who hadn't done much cooking for himself, we all teased him about the way he made spaghetti. He threw pasta into cold water and boiled it to smithereens. Then he poured refrigerator-cold spaghetti sauce directly onto the pasta and started eating. Wade, who is a great cook, gave Lyle a few tips about boiling the water first and heating the sauce before he put it on the pasta.

Some nights we even shared our food. Wade would make a fabulous salad and I'd fix a casserole. Lyle always offered his spaghetti. But more important than the food were the lively conversations around my big dining room table as four or five of us sat down to eat together.

When Ron and Wade left for a couple of weeks of simulator training in another city after their ground school, they both asked if they could come back and stay at my house until the end of the summer, when they could get their families moved to Milwaukee. I said, "Yes, of course!" By now we'd become great friends, and I'd even met their wives and children when they came to visit for a weekend or two.

As each pilot moved his family to Milwaukee after ground school ended, they spread the word about the "Lorenz Crash Pad" to other pilots who asked if they could stay with us. By the second year we had six "crash padders": Lyle, Bob, Dave, Eric, Rob, and Teresa. When Teresa's in town, she sleeps upstairs in the combination sewing/guest room.

All of our "crash padders" decided not to move their families to their home base of Milwaukee and only need a "crash pad" one or two nights a week, unless they're on reserve; then they might be here five nights a week for a month or so.

These days I can't imagine life without the pilots. In addition to the fun they've brought into our lives, I don't have to worry about the house, the mail, or the yard when Andrew and I leave town for a weekend or weeks at a time.

And talk about great role models! Every so often Lyle takes Andrew out to work on his car, something I'd never be able to teach my son. Bob and Andrew enjoy the same kind of movies, and I often hear them laughing and talking together down in the family room. They worked on plans for a tree house and put the thing together one week when Bob was on reserve.

One time I went down to the family room on a weekday morning, and Bob was vacuuming the whole downstairs.

"Bob, what are you doing that for? You don't have to vacuum."

"Aw, it's OK. I'm on reserve and I'm bored. Besides, you're having that party tonight. Thought I'd make myself useful."

I had to jumpstart my heart and then couldn't wait to tell Bob's wife, Mary, the next time I talked to her on the phone about what a thoughtful husband she has.

Dave, who lives in Philadelphia with his wife Barb, is Catholic, and our shared faith gives us lots to talk about. Dave also keeps us informed about the antics of his first child, born while Dave was in ground school.

Eric and his wife and son live in Michigan. Eric's easygoing personality and great sense of humor make spending an evening with him in the family room watching a movie a fun adventure for both Andrew and me.

In addition to flying with the Air National Guard, Teresa is a former math teacher, who, when Andrew needed help the most, was there to hunker down over a page full of algebra problems with him.

When I look back on the years before our crash pad started, I remember many lonely nights in my big family room without a sound in the house. Now, fifteen or twenty nights a month, our home is alive with laughter, conversation, and the best role models I could have asked for my son.

Not only that, but two of my best women friends now are Sharon and Heather, wives of Wade and Rusty, who both moved their families to Milwaukee after their ground school ended. Without a doubt, this experience has opened up our lives to lots of new friendships and warm, wonderful feelings.

There's a verse in Hebrews that puts it all into perspective. It says, "Don't forget to be kind to strangers, for some who have done this have entertained angels without realizing it!" (Hebrews 13:2).

I'll tell you one thing, the "Lorenz crash pad" is definitely a place where the angels we're entertaining have provided us with a lot more than we've given them. But I guess that's just how it works when you step out in faith and open up your home and your heart to strangers.

THE ADOPTION OF
GRANDMA SARAH

~~~

"It'll be great!" I said to my four children. "Just like having a real grandma! We'll have her over for Sunday dinners and introduce her to our friends. She never had any children of her own. Imagine how lonely she must be!"

As I finished tossing the salad for supper, my mind was on the Adopt-a-Grandparent program sponsored by our church. It sounded like such a marvelous idea for my family. The children's grandparents lived hours away in another state, and I felt we definitely needed a hometown grandma.

I could already smell spicy gingerbread cookies baking in her oven. I imagined sitting in her living room in an old cane rocker listening to stories about her girlhood days.

Visions of turning her life around for the better danced before my eyes. I would fix a little extra food once or twice a week and provide her with some good home-cooked meals. And that knitted shawl that had belonged to my mother... wouldn't it be just the thing for our new grandma?

I told my best friend, "Think of the advantages the children are going to receive! They'll learn to care about older people and to make time for them. They'll learn all about the 'olden days.' Maybe she'll teach them how to bake those wonderful German pastries. The director told me her name is Sarah. She was born in Germany in 1890!"

My friend started to say something, but I kept rambling. "And she can teach the girls how to crochet. I'm sure she does that sort of thing. All grandmas do!"

The day finally arrived when we were to meet Grandma Sarah. She lived by herself in an apartment complex for the elderly.

The five of us crowded into her tiny living room. Hats, coats, scarves, and gloves were piled in a mountainous heap on one chair in her closet-sized kitchen.

I spoke first. "Sarah, we're so glad to have you for our grandma. Would you like to come to our house for dinner next Sunday? And if you need to do any shopping, I'll be glad to take you this week." I was blabbering with enthusiasm, hoping it would rub off on the children.

Sarah pushed back a stray curl of white hair and tried to tuck it into the neat twist on top of her head. She spoke slowly, precisely. "My dear, I broke my hip last winter, and I don't go out in the cold anymore. I'm afraid I might fall again. But I don't mind. It's not important to me to get out."

"Oh, goodness." It was all I could mutter. "But what about church? Can't we at least take you to church with us?" I was determined to get her on our social calendar.

"No, not even that. Never missed a Sunday for nearly ninety years, but since last winter I don't even go to church anymore. Two nice folks from the visitation committee bring me communion every Sunday. So I don't mind not going. And I watch services on TV."

"Well then, we'll just have to figure out something else to do together. How about games? Do you play Monopoly or checkers? I noticed the lounge area down the hall with the game tables."

"My eyes, they just aren't what they used to be. Can't read the newspaper anymore. I listen to the radio a lot, though. And those big-print magazines are fine. But games? No. Just can't see well enough. I'm almost ninety-three, you know!"

Sarah was starting to get to me. The more enthusiastic I was about trying to make her life happier and more fulfilling, the more she seemed to cut me off at every pass.

"Well, we'll just visit you then, and talk!" Out of the corner of my eye I saw Jeanne counting the tiles on the ceiling. Julia was fidgeting with the buttons on her sweater.

I continued: "The girls can come over after school some days. Maybe you can teach them to knit or crochet?"

Before Sarah could answer, I hurried on. "And Michael likes to walk to the shopping center next to your apartment with his best friend. They can stop in to see you every Saturday. You know how boys like cookies and milk from Grandma!"

Sarah pulled a bright orange, brown, and gold afghan over her knees. She eyed Michael, who was writing his name on the steamy living room window with his finger. "Well, I do get lots of company. My sister comes every week. And my niece. I have the nicest niece. Reminds me of you, my dear. About your age too. Five kids though. Her oldest just got married. Here, I'll show you the pictures."

At that moment, my youngest, Andrew, announced that he wanted a drink. He ran after Sarah, who was searching for the wedding pictures. Before I could grab him he'd knocked a plant off the coffee table. Jeanne shot me one of those "it's time to get out of here" looks. I cleaned up the potted plant mess, then hustled the children into the kitchen for their coats.

"I'll come back and visit you this week, Sarah. Andrew still takes an afternoon nap and he's getting tired."

"Well, I wouldn't know. Never had any children of my own. Just watched my nieces and nephews grow up from a distance. Haven't had any experience as a grandma. The church folks must have felt that I needed this program. Actually, I'm not a bit lonely. And I sure don't know a thing about being a grandma."

"You're doing great. It'll all work out," I muttered while I fiddled with Andrew's jacket. "Oh, I almost forgot. We brought you some presents. A canned ham, a candle, and this shawl that belonged to my mother."

Sarah looked at the gifts and responded curtly, "My, what will I ever do with that much ham! It'll go to waste. I get Meals on Wheels. They bring my food every noon and there's always plenty left over for supper. I'm not supposed to use my stove. Everyone's afraid I'll burn the place down, I guess."

She chuckled for the first time, then went on. "But you know, I don't miss it. Baking, schmaking. Who needs all that work? Now I relax. You take the ham home. Your big family needs it. And the shawl, too. Dear, I have a drawerful. And the candle. It's lovely, but please, take it. I give most of my things away. Too much work dusting and cleaning everything. When you're as old as I am, you'll want life simple, too."

On the way home hot tears rolled down my cheeks. "How could she be so heartless! She wouldn't even accept our gifts!" I whined to no one in particular.

"Mom," Jeanne answered, "Sarah doesn't seem to be too lonely, and she's certainly not helpless. She seems pretty content to me. I don't think she needs anyone else in her life."

"Of course she needs people in her life! We all do! And this grandparent program is a wonderful opportunity for her. She needs us! She just doesn't know it yet."

Later that afternoon I was reading the church bulletin and noticed the announcement about the Adopt-a-Grandparent program. They used a verse from the Bible to make their point. "Rise in the presence of the aged, show respect for the elderly..." (Leviticus 19:32). I decided that Sarah not only needed us, but that it was my duty to show respect for her as best I could.

Three days later, my spirits and optimism renewed, I popped in on Grandma Sarah. Six nuns, all in short black dresses and veils, were also there to greet me.

Sarah explained, "My one sister, she's a nun, you see, and these are her friends. They visit me every week."

I stopped over once again the next Saturday. This time I interrupted a visit by Sarah's niece and her son. They were just sitting down to an impromptu lunch of cold cuts and deli salads that her niece had brought.

Sarah was cordial enough. When she introduced me to her niece, she said, "This is the lady whose children adopted me as their grandma. Imagine, me, a grandma!"

Sarah tried to find room for me at the tiny kitchen table. I told her I'd already eaten and that I'd wait in the living room. As I turned around she handed me a box of pictures. "Here, look at these. It's the Christmas party the landlord had for all of us here at the apartment," she said. "We have a party every month."

I settled into the overstuffed sofa, let the afghan fall around my shoulders, and basked in the warmth of the room. I fumbled through the pictures. In every one Sarah was surrounded by laughing, happy people. I gazed at these pictures of happiness and listened to the bright chatter between Sarah and her niece.

Was this a sad, lonely old woman? Indeed not. Sarah's life was already filled with love, with people, with small adventures and happy memories. Incredibly alert and healthy for her age, she was enjoying the last years of her life. What right did I have to interfere?

As I reflected on this, I realized that I had actually been *taking away* some of her rights. She had a right to her privacy, a right to choose her own friends, a right to be alone when she wanted, a right to continue depending upon those she felt most comfortable with.

The verse from Leviticus came back to me: "Rise in the presence of the aged, show respect for the elderly..."

Now I knew I wasn't showing Sarah respect at all. I was not respecting what she wanted. At last I began to understand that it was I who was in need. I had been willing to include her in some of my family activities with the hope of receiving so much more. I expected monumental gifts from Sarah... her precious time, her talents, the wisdom of her years, her influence upon my children, and the tales of her past. I wanted her love, her devotion, and her gratitude.

It was time to go. Gently, I refolded the warm afghan and placed it on the back of the sofa. I didn't want to say goodbye to Sarah for good, but when I gave her a hug that day, I knew it was the beginning of a less frequent, less demanding friendship. Sarah had earned her peaceful, contented lifestyle, and I would never play havoc with that again.

LESSONS FROM A COUNTRY GRANDMA

〜〜〜

Agnes, my husband's grandmother, was eighty-five years old when I met her. I was twenty-five. I lived in a big city, St. Louis, with a million other people. Agnes lived in an eye-blinker town in southern Illinois, population six hundred. She'd been a widow for over thirty years, and the way she carried on her single life has always been an inspiration to me.

These days, whenever I feel sorry for myself or even feel a little lonely, I think about Agnes and remember that having a mate isn't everything. I remember one visit in particular, the one I recall every time I see a green, healthy philodendron.

"Agnes, are you sure there isn't something I can do? Peel the potatoes? Make a salad?" I asked the slender, white-haired kitchen dynamo.

Agnes looked up from the sizzling roast she was browning and said matter-of-factly, "No, I'll do that. I guess you *could* water the plant if you *insist* on being useful. Use the jar under the sink. I'm going out to the garden for tomatoes and cucumbers. Don't overdo it with the plant. It needs a drink, not a drowning."

She was out the door in a flash, her apron flying. I filled the oversized fruit jar with well water from the tap and bent down to quench the philodendron. Over the years Agnes had trained the green and white variegated plant to grow up a six-foot strip of wood, then back down again. Then up again on another strip and back down. The day I was there watering it, eight strips of wood supported the philodendron's solid wall of leaves that tapered down into an enormous pot of dirt. As I watered the plant and rearranged a few of the stems, I thought about Agnes.

On the way to meet her for the first time, I'd asked, "What do people do in a town this size? How can anyone stand to live here? There's nothing to do! No culture, no social life, nothing!"

My husband smiled, remembering his childhood days in this tiny town. "You'll see. Wait until we get there."

Agnes' white frame house, where she'd lived for the last sixty-five of her eighty-five years, was just a hoot and a holler (as the townspeople called it) from the town square, four or five blocks away... just far enough for Agnes to justify driving her old gray '48 Plymouth into town to get her week's supply of groceries.

Agnes had never driven a car until she was in her mid-fifties, right after her husband died. She decided the day after the funeral that she would get by on her own even if it meant learning to drive.

For the next thirty years, not a day went by that Agnes didn't drive somewhere: to church meetings, country picnics, friends' houses, or one of the nearby towns to shop. Each year she convinced the folks at the driver's license bureau that she was able and willing to abide by all the rules of the road, and so they kept renewing her license, even into her ninth decade.

The street in front of Agnes' house was paved, but there were no curbs, gutters, or sidewalks. An enormous oak tree that stretched way past the rooftop in her front yard was surrounded by smooth rocks and boulders. Agnes loved to brag about dragging those rocks home from every state in the union while she and her husband, Herb, were on vacations. From sea to shining sea, Agnes insisted that Herb stop the car so she could collect, not a butterfly or a postcard souvenir, but rocks and boulders bigger than watermelons to take home to grace her towering oak.

Just then, Agnes bounded in the screen door, arms filled with garden produce.

"How long have you had this philodendron, Agnes?" I asked.

"Can't remember not having it. Twenty, maybe twenty-five years, I suppose. It's the soil. And the slop bucket," she answered matter-of-factly.

"The what?" I asked, wondering how many other things I didn't understand about "country" life.

Agnes replied with a smile. "All my inedible leftovers and garbage I put in the slop bucket under the sink. Everyday I pour it on the garden. Makes natural fertilizer. Best dirt in the country. Every year or so I add a cupful of that garden dirt to the philodendron. Must like it. Sure grows, doesn't it?" Agnes stepped away from her salad preparations to admire the plant.

That plant was indeed a monument to Agnes' talents. Her friends and relatives were forever clipping off a stem here and there to take home to root in a glass of water. They all wanted their own showpiece plant in twenty years or so.

While Agnes tended to her roast, I stepped onto the back porch. Agnes said she enjoyed living alone. But when her relatives—daughter and son-in-law, four grandchildren and their spouses, and seven great-grandchildren—came home for a visit, she opened up her house and her heart with a graciousness that rivaled that of a fine hotel.

Agnes' white frame house was unassuming but comfortable, filled with the energies of a remarkable woman. She was a woman who, even in her mid-eighties, tended to her garden with fury. A woman who was often out hoeing at 6 A.M.

Agnes cleaned the leaves out of her gutters every spring, mostly, I suspect, because she enjoyed the scolding she received from her friends and neighbors when they discovered that she'd done it once again without asking for help.

Agnes was a sweeper and raker of leaves, a shoveler of snow, a planter of flowers, a mower of grass. Not a season passed without her direct involvement in Mother Nature's dealings.

At age eighty-five Agnes was happy, self-sufficient, and a liver of life. She tackled her daily routine with vigor. She attended church with a passion and firmly believed that the Woman's Christian Temperance Union was next to godliness. She cared for and worried about her daughter, grandchildren, great-grandchildren, and every aunt, uncle, sister, brother, niece, nephew, and cousin in three generations and six counties.

Agnes's house was a quiet place of peace, of simple pleasures, and of the healthiest, biggest philodendron I've ever seen. After that visit with Agnes, I understood what folks do who live in small towns, and why someone, anyone, would want to live in a town like the one Agnes called home.

When I'm eighty-five, I hope I'm just like her.

FIRST DATE

~

"Mom, you realize this is my first REAL date?"

"What about homecoming last year? That was a date."

"That was awful. Formal clothes, parents gawking and taking pictures, slow dancing. It wasn't like going out and really having fun. It was… well, anyway, THIS is a date."

"But you don't know these boys." (At least it was going to be a double date, with Jeanne's best girlfriend, Amy, going along.) "They could be drug addicts, delinquents, potheads. They could be from broken homes." (Before those last words even left my mouth, I winced. I was a single parent, for heaven's sake!) "Where do they go to school?"

"We met them at the forensics meet. They both go to the specialty school for the collegebound in downtown Milwaukee. Mother, they take calculus!"

A week later the doorbell rang. In walked my daughter's girlfriend with the two strangers. One was a youthful clone of Ward Cleaver, from "Leave It To Beaver" fame, a nice-looking boy in a brown plaid sport shirt and gray-rimmed glasses. He looked like he loved calculus.

The other one was dressed all in black, ("He always wears black, Mom. It's OK, it's cool.") including a black leather vest over a black shirt and pants, black fingerless gloves, black sunglasses (including the lenses), and black shoes. A dangly silver appendage hung from his ear like an exclamation point, completing the ensemble. Sort of a cross between Johnny Cash and Ozzie Osbourne

Thank goodness Jeanne's father isn't here to see this. Lord, please, help me say the right things. And Lord, PLEASE don't let this one be Jeanne's date!

My eyes riveted to his hair, which looked like it had been dyed burnt red and then cut with a lawnmower and moussed with thick, black machinery grease so it stood up in uneven spikes all over his head. Vincent Price would have loved this look. I was appalled.

Jeanne and I invited Amy, Mr. Plaid Shirt, and The Creature into the living room. By now we were well past the formalities and I was trying my hardest to ask the kinds of questions fathers always ask their daughter's dates. I'd just finished the ones about whether he had a job and was he planning to go to college ("Yes, Ma'am," to both questions) and had delicately broached the subject of his earring.

"Is that a pop-tab from a soda can you're wearing in your ear?" I asked innocently, clutching the arms of my grandmother's antique swing rocker.

In response, the young man (the others called him "Peter") jumped up from the straight-backed cane-bottom chair I'd steered him to earlier.

"No, it's an orchid. Silver. Would you like to see it?" Before I had a chance to answer, he was hovering over my chair, proudly dangling his orchid earring (still attached to his ear) in my face.

"Oh, that's lovely," I whispered, wishing immediately that I hadn't used the word "lovely." It wasn't a man's word, and I wanted to assure myself and the Black Mariah standing before me that I wasn't doubting his masculinity in the least. (Really.) After all, I'd just read an article in the newspaper that said anyone who was offended by men wearing earrings was just not "with it." Men in record numbers, real men, were wearing them with pride and principle. The fad supposedly was passing from "fad" stage to being as natural as donning a wrist watch or sunglasses. (Yeah, right.)

Heaven help us. Oh, Lord, whatever happened to V-neck sweaters, short, brown wavy hair, and penny loafers? What do I do, Lord? Can I actually send my oldest daughter, who is still tied so tightly to my heartstrings, out into the night with this Creature from the Black Lagoon? Lord, are you there?

When I couldn't think of any more questions to ask either boy, I walked the four teens to the front door. Actually I was praying wildly, to myself. *Please, Lord, send a tornado, anything, just don't let my daughter leave the house with this person. I don't know yet what his dad does for a living, whether they go to church, if he likes children and small animals, if he's....*

At the front door I expected to see a Harley Davidson "hog" motorcycle with a double-wide sidecar. My pulse relaxed a little when I saw the older model, brown station wagon sitting in the driveway. *This must be the Ward and June Cleaver family car,* I thought to myself, and again prayed that my daughter would get in the front seat, next to Mr. Plaid Shirt. She did, but he didn't. The black bandit with the silver earring slid behind the driver's seat.

My pulse quickened. *Where are my heart pills?* I wondered. Then I remembered I don't take heart pills.

As Amy and her "date" (how did they figure out who was with whom in such a split second?) climbed in the back seat, she let out a scream. I hopped off the front step, expecting to see... well, God only knows what I expected to see. By the time I reached the car, Mr. Plaid Shirt in the backseat had handed each girl a long-stemmed yellow rose and a peanut-butter-and-jelly sandwich on white bread carefully tucked into a plastic baggie.

While the girls were ooohhing and aaahhing, Mr. No-Fingers-in-His-Gloves turned around to me and smiled. "Peanut-butter-and-jelly sandwiches are the symbol of friendship," he said sincerely.

"Oh. My goodness. I, ah, I didn't know that." I stammered. Suddenly I couldn't think of one reason not to like this young man, earring and all.

"Be home at 11:30," I smiled.

"No problem, ma'am. We have to be home at midnight, and we live at least a half-hour away. We'll have the girls home BEFORE 11:30."

And they did. And I shouldn't have worried about Jeanne's first real date. When they brought her home at 11:15, both boys walked her to the door. And when they said goodbye, she gave each of them a quick hug. (She told me later.)

I've decided there's something about today's teenagers that has my generation beat hands down. They're expressive. They're individuals. They aren't afraid to be different. But then, I've always been a sucker for peanut-butter-and-jelly myself. And, you know, that earring really WAS gorgeous.

MAY I HAVE THIS DANCE?

❧

I'd been a single parent for over a year. Fourteen months of setting up new family routines, getting settled into three part-time jobs, and smoothing out my frazzled emotions. Most of my evenings were spent running my four children all over town for music lessons; football, basketball, and baseball games; religion classes; shopping; and school events. The weeks and months flew by in a daze of never-ending lists of "things to do."

But then, gradually, I started to notice that there were many times when I felt alone and lonely. Nearly every Friday evening when my youngest visited his father and my three teens were off to the high school games with their friends, I'd sit in the family room alone, aching for adult conversation.

One day, my friend Dianne, another single parent, called. "Pat, there's a singles dance tonight at St. Anthony's school hall. Let's go."

"To a dance? I haven't danced in over two years! Dancing with strangers? I couldn't!"

"Pat, you haven't been out of the house without one of the kids in the back seat for over a year. It's time."

After much prodding from my children, who definitely thought it was a "cool" idea for Mom to go to a dance, I decided to go. I put on my navy blue dress and my low-heeled shoes and met Dianne at the church hall. We paid our three dollars and walked inside.

I glanced at the dance floor and at the cafeteria chairs and tables lined up on either side of the large room. I found two empty chairs at a table near the door, making a mental note that a quick getaway would be easier from this spot. At the opposite end of the room there was a young man singing along with the records he was playing on his elaborate sound system.

Records? I thought. *No live band?*

"Dianne, let's get out of here. This looks like a high-school mixer," I whined.

Actually the room was crowded with people of all ages. A few young ones in their twenties, some oldsters in their sixties and seventies, many middle-agers like me. Widows, widowers, divorced, separated, and people who'd always been single. They all looked like they were having a pretty good time.

Some couples were on the dance floor swinging to the oldie-but-goodie 1960s songs; others were visiting with friends; some were buying sodas and munching popcorn. It all looked so comfortable, so friendly. But as I sat there analyzing the situation, I knew that underneath those giddy faces these people were miserable. They *had* to be miserable, because *I* was. How could I possibly sit at this table, make small talk with Dianne, and wait for a man to ask me to dance? It seemed so juvenile—tawdry, almost. After all, I'd been a married woman for over sixteen years (counting both husbands) and had danced only with my spouse during all those years.

Now here I was, waiting for a perfect stranger to ask me to dance. All I wanted to do was sit down and blend into the woodwork, hoping no one would notice me. I was terrified, if you want to know the truth. And the longer I looked at the crowd, the more I realized that none of those men out there were "Mr. Perfect."

Suddenly "Steve" plopped down on a chair at the end of our table. (I knew his name because we were all required to wear first-name-only name tags.) Steve was at least twenty years older than I, short, pudgy, gray-haired, balding, and obviously trying to decide if he should ask me to dance. I caught him looking at me five or six times, but I quickly averted my eyes each time. *Don't let him ask me to dance,* I anguished. *He's old enough to be my father!*

Two or three songs later, after I'd balled up the little paper napkin under my soda into a dozen tiny white pebbles, Steve moved down across the table from me. He smiled weakly, made a little small talk, then asked me to dance. At the moment, dancing with him seemed easier than figuring out an excuse not to, so we danced.

You know what? Steve was an OK guy. A pleasant man, never married, a competent, gentle dancer who had infinite patience with my initial clumsiness. Steve was having such a good time that soon we were chatting like old friends.

Next, Phil, an intense-looking young man in a dark blue plaid shirt and dark-rimmed glasses asked me to dance. On the dance floor, I placed my left hand on his right shoulder when the music started. Suddenly I felt the wind pop out of my diaphragm as Phil's vise-like grip in his version of "cheek-to-cheek" dancing took hold. At one point I realized my right ear was actually hooked underneath his glasses frame.

When Phil asked me a question, I tried to answer, but I couldn't talk. His torture-chamber grip squeezed me a little tighter each time I uttered a sound until I wondered if my face was actually turning blue from lack of oxygen. Within minutes my neck ached from the intense pressure Darth Vader was placing on the right side of my face. Finally the music stopped, and I quickly unlocked his death grip on my back, freed my ear from under his glasses frame, and raced toward the table.

You don't belong here. This is horrible! I scolded myself as I sat down. While giving my neck a quick self-massage I assured Dianne that sorting laundry at home was more fun than this.

The next person who asked me to dance at the first hint of a slow song, after a round of faster tunes from Buddy Holly's era, was Marvin. Marvin's face was talcum-powder pale. Long, straight hair hung in his eyes… eyes that never blinked, arms that never moved but hung straight and stiff at his sides, and a monotone voice that only uttered one sentence, "Care to dance?"

Marvin was scary. I actually wondered if he had a knife in his pocket. *He wouldn't use it in this crowded room, would he? Would he?* I wondered frantically. Marvin walked and danced like he was afraid of dancing, afraid of women, afraid of dim light, afraid of moving at any speed faster than a crawl. I was glad when the music ended, and Marvin glided on alone. In a way I felt sorry for him. The singles dance was probably the best time he'd had all week. I still thought cleaning closets might be more fun, however.

Then along came Tom who, although he was at least fifteen years my junior, must have noticed my full skirt and decided that I liked to dance to the old standard rock and roll tunes. He was right. So we danced to three or four fast songs. Me, reliving the way I danced in high school in the sixties. And Tom, reliving the way his *parents* danced in high school in the sixties. When the set was finished, including Chubby Checker's "Twist" (the best waist-reducing exercise in the world), I looked and felt like a poor soul who just got dunked at the local carnival dunk tank. Salty sweat was running down my face, down the back of my neck, inside my dress, and was forming a wet ring around my waist. I was huffing and puffing so that I couldn't even answer audibly when good old Steve showed up to ask me for another dance. I just fanned myself with my hand and pointed desperately to my oasis spot at the cafeteria table. He understood my plight and asked a sweet-looking grandmotherly type to dance.

By the end of the evening Dianne and I had each danced and talked with six or eight men and we'd met and shared experiences with, a number of other single mothers as well. When we left the school hall at midnight, we guffawed about the whole adventure, stopped off for a chocolate shake, and made plans to attend the NEXT singles dance. After all, we decided, where else could two forty-year-old single parents break the loneliness barrier and have so much innocent fun for three dollars?

Hug Therapy

~~~

Greet one another with a holy kiss.

2 Corinthians 13:12

In many countries around the world, esteemed friends, business acquaintances, and even strangers greet each other with a big hug and a kiss on each cheek.

I've often wondered, "Do we hug each other enough in this country?" Hugs are not only nice, they're needed. If hugs make the healthy healthier and the happy happier, just think what they can do for the unhealthy and the unhappy! We know that hugs make the most secure among us even more secure, but once again, just think what hugs can do for the insecure.

Hugs relieve pain, depression, stress, and tension. Hugging feels good, overcomes fears, and provides stretching exercise if you're short and stooping exercise if you're tall.

A hug does not upset the environment. It saves heat, is portable, requires no special equipment, makes happy days happier and impossible days possible.

A big hug is very good for your self-esteem, generates goodwill, has no unpleasant side effects, no batteries to wear out, no movable parts, and requires no periodic checkups or maintenance whatsoever.

A hug is inflation-proof, non-taxable, and non-polluting. It has no monthly payments, high interest costs, or insurance requirements. A hug is theft-proof and fully returnable. Hugging improves blood circulation and is invigorating and rejuvenating.

A hug is simple, quick, and almost magical in the way it sends an electrical current of love from one body to another.

Do you give and receive enough hugs? Do you hug your children when they leave in the morning or when they come in from playing? Do you hug your college-age kids when they come home for the weekend? Do you hug friends when you get together? Do you hug your parents or grandpa and grandma every time you see them? If not, why not?

Once you start hugging, it'll probably become addictive. The more hugs you give the more you want to give. And you'll be surprised how many people not only welcome your hugs, but will actually look forward to them. And for goodness sake, we single parents need more hugs than anybody (since we don't get daily hugs from a spouse). So it stands to reason, the more hugs we give, the more we'll get!

Start some hug therapy in your family, school, church, and neighborhood today. It's free and is nothing less than a miracle drug.

To get started and to remind yourself daily to become a hugger, you might want to write this reminder on a card and place it over the kitchen sink:

Lord, help me to reach out to others,

to embrace them with open arms and

squeeze them with love.

Help me to give and receive lots of hugs today.

ANDREW FOUND A RAINBOW...
AND SO DID I

"Hi, Mom!" Seven-year-old Andrew reached around my waist in a giant bear hug. I felt something hard press against my middle and noticed a large round metal button pinned to his shirt that said "S.T.A.R." underlined with a bright rainbow. I wondered why the letters had periods after them... but it was time for the ceremony to begin, and I had to take my seat.

Andrew had just spent a whole Saturday at church with Mrs. Konkel and the other teachers and children in the "Rainbows For All God's Children" program, a support group for children in single-parent and step-family homes. Now we parents were joining our children for a special, end-of-the-semester closing ceremony.

When I walked into the church vestibule I was surprised to see a large wedding in progress. As I tiptoed past the two open doors of the church, I glanced in to see a radiant bride, her smiling groom, a whole line of attendants in bright pink dresses, and a church full of delighted observers.

How appropriate, I thought sarcastically. *Here we are at a gathering for children going through the anguish of their parents' broken marriages and just down the hall a wedding is taking place. Another marriage, two people in love. Children will be born, a family begun. Will that marriage also end in divorce like mine had?* I wondered, not surprised by the old familiar bitterness welling up inside me.

Sister Anthony Marie, the coordinator of the Rainbows program, greeted me at a door down the hall. "You're just in time. We had to change rooms because of the wedding. You can sit in that rocking chair over there."

The other parents looked comfortable on the couches and easy chairs lined up along one wall. I glanced around, relieved that my ex-husband and his girlfriend weren't there.

The small room was filled with parents and children, many of whom had plopped down on the carpeted floor just a foot away from Father John. He smiled and nodded as I took my place in an overstuffed rocker.

Sister Anthony Marie spoke first. "One out of every three school-age children now lives in a single-parent home. More than half of all children will go through the agony of losing a parent by divorce, separation, or death. The loss of a parent affects children spiritually, socially, academically, and behaviorally. Many children blame themselves for their parents' divorce and they agonize over their guilt. Children need time and guidance to work through this loss, just as adults do."

As Sister Anthony continued to talk about the Rainbows group, I reflected on the past twenty months since my ex-husband and I had separated... months that I had spent trying to raise three teenagers and a first-grader on my own, trying to keep a large home going inside and out, and trying to keep up with three part-time jobs. Frustration, loneliness, and exhaustion had taken over my life. The children and I had definitely been affected spiritually, socially, and behaviorally.

Earlier that day the children had helped prepare the readings for this ceremony that would close the first semester of the Rainbows program. Sister Anthony asked Kathy, one of the older girls in the group, to read from Corinthians. The words had been paraphrased so the children could better understand their meaning. Kathy brushed away a long wispy curl from the side of her face and began to read in a clear voice:

"My love must be patient. My love must be kind."

My own thoughts darted in between Kathy's words. *I haven't been as patient or as kind as I should be to my children lately. But it's so hard being a single parent!* I rationalized.

Kathy continued. "My love must not be jealous. My love cannot stick its nose in the air. My love must not be rude or selfish. My love must not get angry or fight back."

Hah! Not get angry? How can I help but get angry? I didn't want this divorce. All I wanted was a year's separation so we could work on the problems in the marriage without the day-to-day tension that our living together had created. How did I know that two months after we separated he would file for divorce without even telling me why? Don't I have a right to be angry?

Kathy ended with, "My love must find happiness with those who are happy. My love has no limit. It must never fail."

"Love must never fail"? How can I believe that, when my marriage just failed? We wouldn't be here today if love hadn't failed!

The words Kathy read were jabbing my memory with their pointedness. I thought back to my own wedding, when Andrew's father and I had exchanged vows, and then suddenly I remembered... we had printed the very same passage from the thirteenth chapter of First Corinthians in our wedding booklet. We had read the words aloud, together, at the ceremony.

And now we'd come full circle. Here we were talking about love being patient and kind and enduring forever, in a room full of parents and children torn apart by love that had shattered into broken fragments.

My thoughts were interrupted by the shuffling of papers as the children and parents began to sing from the song sheets. It was obvious that the children had practiced the song during the day because they were belting it out with gusto.

"I believe in the sun, even when it isn't shining.
I believe in love, even when there's no one there.
I believe in God, I believe in God, even when He is silent."[1]

The children seemed so happy. Andrew was beaming from ear to ear as he snuggled closer to his beloved Mrs. Konkel. It was obvious that this Rainbows program had helped bring back a sense of hope and faith to these children. I thought back to six months earlier when I'd first read about it in our church bulletin.

"Rainbows for All God's Children" is a national non-profit organization open to all children of all races and religions. It offers weekly support groups for children living in single-parent families and stepfamilies. Small groups are headed by caring adults who are trained by the Rainbows staff to offer support, understanding, and guidance through presentations, activities, discussions, peer support, and a safe place to share themselves.

Just a week before, Andrew's teacher had called me, saying he'd been acting up in school and seemed to have a lot of angry feelings inside of him.

My heart ached. I had the same angry feelings inside me. Here was this small child trying to keep his real feelings about the divorce hidden from me and his father. But at school those feelings festered, magnified, and spilled out angrily.

So for twelve Saturday mornings, Andrew joined the first-grade Rainbows group headed by Mrs. Konkel, who convinced the children that they were loved and that they were special. She also gave him and the other children in his group the opportunity to openly express, in confidence, the feelings that had been churning inside them.

Within two months not only his teacher at the public school but also the principal and even his Sunday school teacher all commented to me that Andrew seemed much happier, more relaxed, and very cooperative.

I could see it at home, too. He fought less with his siblings. He stopped having temper tantrums. He whined less and hugged me more.

If Andrew could learn to feel special again, why couldn't I? I wondered. Why couldn't I be more like these little children who believe in miracles "even when there's no one there"?

I knew I had an attitude problem. I needed help to get on with my life and to be more like these little children who believe in miracles.

Near the end of the ceremony, it was Andrew's turn to be a star. He stood up, faced everyone in the room, grinned at me, and read from his Rainbows diploma:

"I am me,
There was only one of me created by God.
I was not cut out like a cookie from dough.
I am so special I have my very own fingerprints,
My very own face
My very own body.
I have my own thoughts, dreams, and feelings.
Other people may have different feelings from me.
It is OK not to agree with other people too.
I will make some mistakes and I will try to learn from them.
I will laugh at myself, but will not make fun of others.
I will have fun living inside my skin.
I have value.
I am one of God's children.
I am important.
I am me.
I am special." [2]

Andrew looked right into my eyes as if to say, "You're special, too, Mom. It's time to get happy again!"

Afterwards, when the celebration was over, everyone hugged

everyone else in the room. All those warm, friendly, loving arms squeezed me in a gesture that said, "You are special." I felt an outpouring of love that I hadn't felt in years. When those people, who had been strangers an hour before, opened their arms to me, I felt my bitterness barriers melt away. I knew then that there was hope for love in this world after all.

Andrew and I walked hand in hand out the door and into the sunshine. "Andrew, that's a great button on your shirt. You really are a STAR! But why do they have periods after each letter?"

"That's the Rainbows star, Mom! S.T.A.R. means *Sadness, Then A Rainbow.* But I'm not sad anymore, Mom, are you?"

"No, Andrew, I'm not. I think we're both stars who have found a rainbow!"

Later that week, I signed up for a New Horizon Weekend, a healing experience for separated and divorced men and women, sponsored by the Archdiocese of Milwaukee. With the help of new friends, a more relaxed work schedule, and a determination to stop worrying about money, I was able to work my way out of the bitter feelings that trap so many divorced people.

The following semester Andrew was involved in the second grade "Rainbows For All God's Children" program. Slowly, surely... the Lorenzes became a family once again... a family who loves rainbows.

1. "I Believe in the Sun" by Carey Landry © 1973 by Rev. Carey Landry and North American Liturgy Resources, 2110 W. Peoria Ave., Phoenix, AZ 85029. Used by permission.

2. "I Am Me" from the Rainbows Program Kit distributed by "Rainbows," 1111 Tower Road, Schaumburg, IL 60173. Used by permission.

SOD BUSTER

～～～

The summer of 1988 was the hottest on record in Milwaukee, and the month of June was the second driest June since 1870, with just seven-tenths-of-an-inch of rain. Naturally, a month before that record-breaking drought began, I spent my entire savings on sod. Why would a single parent on a tight budget do such a thing, you might ask?

Well, it's because I knew my home was my only real asset (other than my children, of course), and at the time I felt the best investment I could make in my future was to maintain and preserve my home.

My backyard was a homeowner's nightmare: the abandoned garden had weeds the size of frisbees; the two-foot drop-off from the patio to the trees was an eroded mess of mud and rocks; and the old sandbox pit was now a dirt-and-sand pit three times its original size.

The first of June the landscapers placed the thick, green sod on the newly dug-up and leveled yard. It looked like a golf course. I had visions of *House and Garden* coming to take pictures. They said to water it for a week if it didn't rain. It didn't. So I did. When I had to leave town my neighbors brought over their hoses and sprinklers so there were three fountains spewing fresh water on my new grass.

By mid-June and there was still no rain in sight, those blessed neighbors completely gave up on their own yards which were dry, brown, and parched from the heat and lack of rain, but they made sure the sprinklers continued day and night on my yard. That sod was going to grow roots or else!

By the end of Milwaukee's "hottest and driest summer ever," my yard was still picture-postcard perfect, like a giant emerald dropped on the desert. All summer I was reminded that God often doesn't send down the showers and make the green grass grow like we'd like Him to. But He certainly does give us the means to find other solutions to our problems. Like neighbors and friends who care. Sometimes all we single parents have to do is ask. You'll be surprised how people rally 'round when you ask for their help.

One thing's for certain. That summer of 1988 I learned firsthand that the seeds of the Lord's goodness are planted deep in the hearts of my friends and neighbors.

DOG DAYS

I've often wondered why so many things you read about single parenting include the advice that pets are a great family idea. Do these authors really think a big slobbering St. Bernard is a good substitute for a mom? Or that a yapping, high-strung curly-haired poodle can protect the family like a big husky dad? Get real. To my way of thinking, a dog is just another big hairy expense that most single parents can't afford.

I've never owned a dog and, in fact, am not too crazy about canine creatures. But that's not something you admit to your friends. To be perfectly honest, I can't believe I'm actually doing it here. In this pet-crazed country of ours, disliking dogs is something akin to not liking the American flag or not liking babies.

So when my friend Susie asked if our family would keep Woofer for four days while her family went up north on vacation, I agreed, lest I become known as the neighborhood antidog establishment.

My kids were overjoyed. They'd been begging for a dog for thirteen years. Here was the chance to gratify their basic "animal instincts."

Susie arrived with Woofer Sunday night with his sleeping basket, his favorite chewed-up pink blankie, food and water dishes, canned dog food, and a list a page long of things to do for His Dog-Eared Majesty. She also assured me that Woofer only needed to go out two or three times a day to relieve himself.

Susie said goodbye to the pooch and left me to fend for myself in a new doggy-dog world. Fifteen minutes later, after sniffing every object in our home, Woofer joined the family in the living room and promptly did his business right on the living room carpet. It was the business we referred to in grammar school as "number two."

I was a little miffed, but after I cleaned up the mess, I realized Woofer was probably just confused. I worried about the carpet, then remembered that over the years every conceivable food, liquid, and other substance had been ground into that carpet at one time or another. I decided to forgive and forget.

Next thing I knew, Woofer was standing on three legs in the dining room, spraying the bar stools, which don't look a bit like fire hydrants. I was quickly running out of excuses for Woofer's ungentlemanly behavior.

After I cleaned up that mess and scolded the dog appropriately by yelling my fool head off, I assigned each of the three older children his or her own day for dog duty. Each child would have a turn to walk, feed, exercise, and play with our canine cohort. I also suggested they take him out at least five or six times a day, since Wonder Dog had already amply demonstrated, within an hour, his inability or unwillingness to refrain from relieving himself wherever he pleased.

By morning of day two, the carpet was dry and the county zoo odor had dissipated. Even though Woofer had ignored his basket and pink blankie for his night's sleep, and chosen the good living-room couch instead, I tried to make friends with him. Andrew, having had the same idea, grabbed Woofer by the collar and began to drag him down the hall toward the playroom.

Woofer retaliated by biting the overzealous child on the hand. I comforted Andrew, then assured Woofer that dragging dogs by the neck was not a normal part of our routine.

Jeanne appeared on the scene, furious that some bestial creature had turned over the wastebasket in the downstairs bathroom and left chewed-up tissues and trash all over the place. I smiled gently and reminded her that she had been begging for a dog her entire life and ended my self-serving speech with something profound like, "You have to take the bad with the good."

She stomped off when I reminded her it was her day for doggy duty and she better take him outside before he watered the house plants.

Mealtimes during our dog days were a definite challenge to my sanity. I just wasn't used to having soulful eyes and a wet wagging tongue perched expectantly six inches from my plate. Embarrassed to be eating in front of even a four-legged someone, I gobbled my food, then set the leftovers on the floor for Woofer. He devoured every morsel before I could get back to my chair. Figuring it was my good cooking that Woofer loved, I started to genuinely like that dog.

But right then Michael announced that when he was emptying the wastebaskets downstairs he came to one that was all wet inside and out and smelled to high heaven. This time my patience hit rock bottom. I demanded that the dog-sitter-of-the-day take the mutt outside so he could romp and lift his leg to his heart's content.

The third day passed without a hitch. Woofer was back in my good graces. At lunchtime I even gave him two-and-a-half bowls of my special seafood bisque, a rich cream soup loaded with salmon, tuna, shrimp, and crab. I like it, the kids hated it, and Woofer thought it was divine. After that culinary delight, I couldn't go anywhere without Woofer wagging his tail behind me.

The morning of day four, one of the kids announced that someone had upchucked in the living room. They said it looked like seafood bisque. Woofer looked a little sheepish so I promised never to tempt him into gluttony again. I cleaned up that mess, then suggested someone take His Majesty out for a long walk.

I needed to get away and decided a trip to the grocery store would do me good. While I was gone, Susie and her family returned from Blissful City and retrieved man's best friend from the children. She called later to thank me personally for taking such good care of their dog.

Her very words were, "I'm glad he didn't give you any trouble. The kids said he was really good and that they can't wait to get him back again next year when we go on vacation."

I didn't have the heart to go into any details, so I just said, "Sure, Susie, anytime."

I immediately began to wonder if I could get the house sold and if we could get moved to a different state before their next vacation.

FIFTEEN MOST IMPORTANT WORDS

My dear friend and neighbor, Bruce Swezey, is a pilot with a commercial airline and with the Wisconsin Air National Guard. Bruce is also a Bible scholar who, over the years, has filled my heart and head with the wonder of God's words. One day I asked Bruce, "What are the most important words you ever read or learned?"

Of course I expected something profound from the Bible, but without blinking Bruce said, "The thirty-nine-word bold print 'Emergency Action For Spin Recovery.'" Then he rattled off the thirty-nine words in less than twelve seconds:

Throttles: idle. Rudder and ailerons: neutral. Stick: abruptly full aft and hold. Rudder: abruptly apply full rudder opposite spin direction (opposite turn needle) and hold. Stick: full forward one turn after applying rudder. Controls: neutral and recover from dive.

Bruce had learned this life-saving method of getting an airplane out of a downward spin when he was in pilot's training after he graduated from the Air Force Academy in the seventies. I laughed at his lightning-fast performance and then shared with him the fifteen most important words I'd ever learned.

I told him my fifteen words often help me "recover from a spin" also. They help me get more things accomplished in life. They help me find the answers to many problems. They help me communicate my real feelings to others. They help me get along better with all sorts of people and show my appreciation for them. And they help me maintain a positive attitude no matter how much of a "spin" I'm in. When I try to use them every day, I can really soar!

My fifteen words are actually five words, then four words, three, two and one... and thus, very easy to remember and say every day as often as possible. So here we go: five, four, three, two, one... blast off!

My Fifteen Most Important Words

I Am Proud of You. These five little words make all the difference in the world after a job well done. But how many times do we forget to say them? Funny thing is, when we do say them, they sort of boomerang back to us. That's because when you tell children you're proud of them for a job well done, they almost always work harder to keep your pride in them strong and vocal.

"I am proud of you! You made your bed all week without being reminded."

"I am proud of you! Do you know how much the people you babysit for appreciate the time you spend with their children?"

"I am proud of you! You studied hard and brought that 'D' up to a 'C.'"

What Is Your Opinion? These four words are sure-fire day brighteners to everyone we meet at home, school, work, church, the store, everywhere!

"I'm thinking of buying a new chair for the family room. What is your opinion?"

"My son is having a hard time with algebra, and I'm wondering if he needs a tutor in order to pass your class. What is your opinion?"

"This contract may need some revision. What is your opinion?"

"Pastor Ron, how about a fundraiser to help buy a new piano for church. What is your opinion?"

"Before you fix my lawnmower, I'm wondering if I'd be better off buying a new one. What is your opinion?"

When we genuinely ask for the opinions of those around us, we single parents are suddenly relieved of that heavy feeling that we have to make all the decisions for the entire family, all the time, by ourselves. A little "asked for" advice from our friends, family, neighbors, coworkers, and church members goes a long way.

I Love You. These three little words are actually among the biggest words in the universe. We can never hear them enough. How can we be angry, hurt, depressed, down in the dumps, or ambivalent toward someone who says "I love you" every single day many times a day? Tell your kids every day, in as many ways as you can, I love you, I love you, I love you.

Thank You. Thank you. Gracias. Merci. Danke. In any language, this phrase is a powerful motivator. Teach your children to write thank-you notes for every single gift they receive. Teach them by doing it yourself. The social art of writing our thanks seems to be falling by the wayside, causing a whole generation of youngsters to grow up thinking they have those gifts coming and that a proper, well-thought-out "thank you" isn't necessary. It is! "Thank you" isn't something we just teach our two-year-olds to say after the nice lady gives them a popsicle. "Thank you" is something we say to everyone for everything all our lives. And when we've received an actual gift, even if it's as intangible as a weekend at grandma's house, we need to say "thank you" and write "thank you." Thank you for doing it.

Yes. This may be the single most important word in the world. "Never say no when you can say yes," was the best advice my mother could have ever given me. Life is too short to live cautiously. All through their childhoods I told my children, "Whenever anyone asks you to do anything, automatically say yes, unless you can think of a good reason to say no."

Shortly after my Aunt Helen turned eighty-five, she sent me a short essay written by another eighty-five-year-old woman from Kentucky. That woman's words explain exactly what I'm talking about when it comes to the importance of saying "yes."

If I had my life to live over, I'd dare to make more mistakes next time. I'd relax, I would limber up. I would be sillier than I have been this trip. I would take fewer things seriously. I would take more chances. I would have taken more trips. I would have climbed more mountains.

You see, I've been one of those persons who lived sensibly and sanely hour after hour, day after day. I've never gone anywhere without a thermometer, a hot water bottle, a raincoat, a parachute. If I had to do it over again I would have traveled lighter.

If I had my life to live over, I would go barefoot earlier in the spring, and stay that way later in the fall. I would go to more dances. I would ride more merry-go-rounds. I would pick more daisies.

I would perhaps have had more actual troubles, but I'd have had fewer imaginary ones.

So, I leave you with my fifteen most important words. I believe they should be declared the official "Single Parent's Creed" because the more we say them, the more optimistic and happy we'll become.

I AM PROUD OF YOU,
WHAT IS YOUR OPINION?
I LOVE YOU.
THANK YOU.
YES.

"THE SWILL GANG"

～～～

I closed the curtains in my family room, flipped the TV channels, and settled into my green rocker for another night of solo TV watching when the phone rang. It was a woman named Sunny calling from Valdosta, Georgia.

"I just read something you wrote in *The Single Parent* magazine, and I have to talk to you. I'm a single parent, too, and sometimes I just don't know if I can make it on my own. I thought it would help to talk to someone else who's raising children alone."

We talked for an hour, and Sunny continued to call every couple of weeks. Actually, we sort of commiserated with each other because that year, 1989, was the worst of my life.

It was the year the man I'd dated for ten months suddenly moved to Oklahoma to start a new career.

It was the year my nine-year-old son, Andrew, was devastated by his father's death.

It was the year my oldest daughter, Jeanne, got caught in the middle of the California earthquake, and I lived through nightmarish days wondering if she was safe.

The year 1989 was the year my eighteen-year-old daughter, Julia, graduated from high school and decided to spend the summer before college testing my sense of "loving motherhood." We hollered and picked at each other all summer. I'm not sure if the thought of leaving home for the first time to go to college had her befuddled, or if I just couldn't get used to the idea of first Harold, then Jeanne, and now Julia leaving us. Many nights that year my family room felt like an empty auditorium as I sat alone with the TV set.

After more long-distance phone calls from Sunny, she told me she wanted to move back to the northern part of the U.S.

(her original home) so I invited her to Milwaukee for a week-end to attend a conference for single people. She stayed for a week and bought a house while she was here. She kept calling me her "best" friend even though I was wallowing too deep in my own miseries to be anybody's "best" anything.

But as a favor to Sunny, after she made the move with her two young daughters, I decided to gather some of my women friends to meet her. I called every woman I knew... friends from church, from work, from the neighborhood. Friends I met over the years through other people. Mothers of my children's friends. A couple from my writing club.

I was a bit nervous at first, inviting them to my house all at once, knowing that few of them knew each other. I introduced everyone as they arrived, and before long we were talking, laughing, and gabbing like old friends about our jobs, children, and lifestyles.

Sunny commented, "The women I knew in southern Georgia were generally described as 'precious.' You people aren't just 'precious,' you're downright interesting!"

That was it... the thread that wove us together. We were "interesting" women.

Tina piped up, "I think we should do this every month! Let's call it the Southeastern Wisconsin Interesting Ladies League. S.-W.-I.-L.-L."

I laughed. "SWILL! SWILL? We're going to form a club and call it SWILL?"

"Why not?" Sharon asked. "We can gather together and just unload all the 'swill' that creeps into our lives periodically and get support from each other."

And so we began at the end of 1989. We decided to meet at my house every month since I had the largest family room and the fewest family members to uproot on Friday nights.

We kept it simple. SWILL had only one rule. Whatever confidences, problems, or heartaches were discussed in that family room during our SWILL meetings stayed in that room. We trusted each other, cared about each other, and helped each other if possible.

I never worried about cleaning the house before a SWILL meeting because nobody was there to do a white-glove inspection. And I didn't worry about fancy refreshments. If one of us was having a chocolate or salty foods craving, we brought a bag of candy or pretzels to toss on the coffee table to share. But we resolved from the beginning never to get bogged down, as some clubs do, with a "fancy food" complex.

Over the years at least thirty women have woven their way in and out of the SWILL meetings. Anyone can bring an interesting friend to the meetings, and if that friend likes us, she can come forever. Sometimes we've had a dozen at one time, and other months, because of hectic schedules, only three or four.

But it doesn't matter how many. What matters is that as we get to know each other, we begin to care more and more about each other. We are, after all, a family.

SWILL welcomes everyone regardless of age, race, religion, or occupation. Everyone from Laurie, a young married woman in her late twenties with four small children, struggling with the possibility of her marriage ending... to Eunice, who's been married for forty-five years and taken enough college-level classes in her retirement to be one of the most interesting people in the group.

When one of our group, Linda, died of heart failure at age thirty-nine after only meeting with us a short time, we mourned together. We discussed ways to solve the medical insurance problems that often face single, overstressed parents like Linda, who worked three jobs to make ends meet.

When Jody's teenage son, Daniel, died in a car accident, we held each other and cried with Jody at the funeral.

When Ann shared with us that her ex-husband had become a street person to avoid child support, we encouraged her to go back to court to get her "ex" some disability funding which would include child support for her. She did and the SWILL members were her biggest cheerleaders.

When Gail, who had gone back to school to study nursing, decided she wanted to quit, we spent hours talking her into staying in school. One of our members, a counselor, helped Gail through some test anxiety problems one night. Gail graduated from nursing school in 1992, and we all took a bow.

When Barb's son came home from Desert Storm and moved back into her "empty nest" home, we listened... and listened some more when a few months later her daughter moved back home with her new baby. We heard about the ups and downs of Barb's four-adults-in-one-house, three-generation family. We gave her lots of advice, including the fact that it was OK for her to go back to work full time.

Carol, whose happy marriage rubs off on all of us, points out that even a happy marriage isn't perfect all the time, but that a wonderful sense of humor can get you through most of the "swill" that marriage can dish out.

Sunny became much more independent; found a wonderful job as a school counselor; made lots of new friends at work, in her neighborhood, and in her church; and moved on to start her own support network.

What did SWILL do for me... the one who was simply trying to find a few friends for Sunny? I'm the one who benefited the most. These women who are single, separated, divorced, and married, and who come from all walks of life, open their hearts and their lives to me, month after month. They listen to me, laugh with me, and help me through the rough times of being a single parent. When I had three children in college at once and a fatherless twelve-year-old at home, they helped me even more through the struggles by offering financial advice as well as emotional help. I've learned to talk about my fears and my failures and to admit that I'm scared at times and that it's OK to have conflicts with the ones you love.

I've also learned how important it is to get out of the house and get plenty of exercise. Gail and I started rollerskating two or three times a week on the bike path near Lake Michigan. And Betsy and I took long walks nearly every Saturday until she moved to a different neighborhood. I lost a few pounds in the process and felt better physically than I had in a long time.

One thing's for sure. The years that have followed 1989 have been better by far because of the "interesting" and loving women friends I made through SWILL.

These days I'm just wondering if we shouldn't change our name to SWELL. Because we are. A swell bunch of women who, over the years, have become a family to each other, a non-judgmental support system that's always there on the first Friday of each month. Whether we have too much stress in our jobs, have a child going through a painful divorce, are planning a career change, are looking for advice on how to have better communication with a spouse, or just need a night out away from the daily grind, SWILL is there.

Once again the good Lord has filled my family room with "family." A new family of friends. It's amazing how much love I feel now that I've learned to open my life to these friends and to nourish that friendship on a regular basis.

How To Support Your Friends

So now that you know all about the "Southeastern Wisconsin Interesting Ladies League," perhaps you'd like some down-to-earth suggestions on how to start your own support group.

All of us at one time or another need the support of others as we go through different stages of our lives. Loneliness, starting a new career, living in an unhappy marriage, going through a divorce, learning to cope as a single parent, feeling caught between caring for children and elderly parents, having your last child leave home, or struggling with financial or emotional problems of any sort... all are examples of rough times that a support group can help ease. Starting such a group is very simple.

1. Invite anyone and everyone. I once received a letter from a woman in Tucson who asked how to start a support group "for middle-aged, divorced women whose children are gone and who are facing life alone." What you DON'T want to do if you're in that situation is surround yourself just with people who are in the same situation. Whoa! What a downer that would be!

What you need is to be with people of all ages, religions, ethnic backgrounds, careers, and marital situations. Divorced people need to know that many marriages are truly happy. Married people need to know that divorce is terribly painful and that those going through it need lots of help. Younger people need to know how interesting and wise older folks are. And older people need to be pepped up by what the younger ones are doing. "Variety is the spice of life" is definitely more than just a quaint adage when it comes to starting a support group.

2. Keep it simple. Our SWILL group meets once a month, always on the first Friday of the month, always at my house at 7:30. I NEVER get stressed out knowing I have a family room full of guests coming because I NEVER bother to do a "special" housecleaning for it and I NEVER worry about snacks. Whoever feels like bringing something to munch on does. Some nights we "feast" on a bag of red licorice and Barb's homemade caramel corn, or Carol's famous taco dip and chips. But food isn't and should never be the important thing. You're there to talk and listen, not to eat.

3. Avoid gossip. The members of your support group should always feel that they can share whatever events, burdens, or problems they have with the other members of the group without worrying about whether so-and-so's husband or the members' outside friends will be "talking" about what was shared at the support group. Your number one rule should be simply: WHAT IS SHARED IN THE GROUP STAYS IN THE GROUP.

4. Listen as a group. One other guideline we have at SWILL is that only one person is supposed to talk at a time. Some nights we may only have five or six members present, but other months there may be a dozen or more. When the group gets large, it's tempting to break off into splinter conversations. But if you ask the members to please stay with the main group, everyone will have a chance to listen and to share advice when appropriate. It helps if you can arrange the chairs in your living or family room in a big oval or circle so that no one feels left out.

5. Begin with a "round table." The best way to get things going and to keep them moving is to start on one side of the room and simply let each person talk for a few minutes about what is happening in his or her life. Before you know it, the conversation is going full blast with lots of sharing, caring, laughing, and advice giving. Just make sure that everyone gets a chance to speak. As hostess I try to make sure each person in the circle gets her turn. Sometimes when we're doing the "round table," we may get off on a completely different subject. When that happens, I'll say something like, "Hey, that sounds really interesting, but let's finish our round table before we get back to that. So, what's going on in your life, Jane?"

Supporting one another by simply getting together and talking about our lives, our loves, our jobs, and our problems is the most healthful way to relieve stress. One thing's for sure: After each SWILL meeting, and after all the hugs at the front door, the members of our group walk away knowing that they have a roomful of friends who really care about them, friends who are there 365 days a year if necessary.

MOM'S GOT A DATE TONIGHT!

~~~

When I first became a single parent, I felt like my head was caught in the eye of a tornado with both feet dangling and my arms flailing.

But I also knew that I was from solid, strong-as-an-oak-tree stock and that I had four children to care for, a large house to maintain, and three part-time jobs to coordinate. It was a hectic time, to be sure, and my social life was a blur of activity.

"Hey, Mom, would you mind if a few of my friends came over for a little party? If you could just fix the food and then stay upstairs while we're down in the family room, it'd be great!"

"Mom, can you drive me to Kelly's house? And then when you pick me up, could we run out to the shopping center to look for new cheerleading shoes?"

"You're going to the game tonight, aren't you, Mom? I might get to play a couple minutes like last time."

"Mommy, can we go sledding? On the big hill? Please, Mom? There's lots of new snow!"

Yes, indeed, my social life was a whirl all right. Not exactly your basic adult-type events, mind you, but always on-the-go, something-to-do-every-minute, no-time-for-depression activities, to be sure.

Then one day it happened. A man who owned a restaurant for which I had been writing radio commercials called and invited me to dinner. I wasn't sure I was ready to get dressed up and make "small talk" with a man I hardly knew, but because my children thought the idea of mom having a "date" was practically the next-best-thing to having a dad in the home, they talked me into accepting.

I met the gentleman at his restaurant, we dined luxuriously, took a walk, and then I drove home. Jeanne, who was seventeen at the time, was waiting up for me. "So Mom, tell me all about him. Did you have fun?"

"Well, my dear, if you want to know the truth, he was too old, too short, too rich, and drank too much to suit my tastes."

"Mother, you're never going to find a man with that attitude," Jeanne quipped.

Find a man? Was that what I was trying to do? No, of course not. I wasn't looking for another relationship. I was just starting to get used to the idea of being "head of the household" and I rather liked the responsibility. I even liked learning how to use an ax to split wood for my wood burner and then rev up the chain saw to cut the wood down to size. On those days my 5'7" frame felt as tall as Paul Bunyan... and after a weekend of that sort of activity, who had the energy to smile politely, let alone look for a date?

But a year later, after putting over fifteen thousand miles on my little car running the kids all over kingdom come with their myriad of activities... it happened again. My second "date."

I met this gentleman at work also, and our dinner date was pleasant enough. But, he, too, had children almost my age, and he seemed more interested in golf and tennis than anything else in the world, including dinner with me. And since I don't play golf or tennis, we were doomed from the start.

"Mom, that's what you said about your date last year! You're too picky. Do you like being single?"

As a matter of fact I did. During the next year I found other things to do during my "free" time. I ushered for musicals at a Milwaukee theater with another single mother, then watched the performances "on the house." I joined the religious education committee at church and did some volunteer writing for a local Christian singles magazine. Andrew and I made some new friends when we joined a single parents' and children's group that met for dinner and discussion on Tuesday nights.

On Fridays we went to the high-school games to watch Michael play basketball and Julia cheerlead. On Saturdays we rented movies, popped popcorn, and relaxed at home.

My life was full. Purposeful. Meetings, activities, and the children filled the void in my life, and I went to bed exhausted and amazingly content... every night.

"Pat," my happily married friend, Carol, said one day, "there's a 'Single Again' group at church. Maybe you'll meet somebody there."

"I know, Carol, I've already joined the group. Last month we all went out for a fish fry, twenty-five women and one man. But that's OK, I'm still having fun with my kids, honest."

The next year another friend called. "You have to meet Ben. He's single, your age, no kids, and wants to meet someone who likes quiet evenings at home watching movies on the VCR. He doesn't go out much, but he's very good about fixing things around the house. You might like him."

Might I like him because he's a handyman? What sort of personality trait is that? I wondered. But I also caught myself wondering if he'd be good with landscaping or fixing the snowblower.

Ben came over one Saturday afternoon. We talked for a couple of hours. Then I said, "Well, I really do have to run some errands this afternoon." My mental translation of that statement was something like, *I would honestly rather run errands than spend another hour thinking up things to talk to you about, so if you don't mind, would you please leave now?*

Ben stood up quickly and said, "I'll come with you and then we can rent a movie to watch later on."

Just as the movie began, my children started coming home. Julia from her babysitting job, Andrew from visiting his dad's house, and Michael from his job as stock boy at a local pharmacy.

So there we were in the family room. Me, in my big green chair next to the woodburner. Ben on the couch next to my chair. Andrew next to Ben, Julia next to Andrew. Michael plopped down on the love seat. A few minutes later Tony and John (Michael's friends) came over and squeezed in on the couch and loveseat.

Well now. Wasn't this cozy. Mom, her date, eight-year-old Andrew, and four teenagers. Michael kept looking at me sort of funny, like, "Where did you find this one, Mom?" I felt like I was on trial. Ben stood up, rubbed his slicked-back hair, and went over to investigate the innards of the wood burner again. He liked that contraption, obviously more than he liked being in a room full of jovial teens, a hip-and-trendy second grader, and a woman who yawned a lot.

I wondered what the children thought of him, and I secretly wished he'd go home so I could put on my lounging pajamas and get comfortable. I also wanted to read the paper and write a letter to my folks. But instead I had to sit there and entertain this humorless gentleman who was probably thinking to himself that he didn't expect a crowd when he asked if he could come over and get acquainted.

Oh Lord, I know my friends and I have been grumbling about my "meeting a nice man" off and on for three years. And now, here's one sitting in my family room, and I can hardly wait until he goes home! Why am I so fickle, Lord? Do I really need or want to find someone special and get married again?

Those thoughts kept flitting through my head during the entire nine hours that Ben stayed at our house that Saturday. When he finally left at midnight after two-and-a-half movies, a pizza, and a houseful of kids coming and going, I had to admit that being with someone just for the sake of being with someone can be a lot worse than sitting home alone.

So what if my friends, coworkers, and even my children think my goal in life should be to find a nice man and settle down? I know in my heart that I'm not ready for that... and maybe I never will be. At least for now, the man of my dreams, the one who is easygoing, strong, sensitive, has a great sense of humor, and a deep faith... just hasn't come around yet... and maybe he never will.

If he doesn't, it's OK. I keep remembering something I read in Luke 11:36:

> If you are filled with light within, with no dark corners, then your face will be radiant too, as though a floodlight is beamed upon you.

These days that "light within" makes me feel very good about myself because that light comes from God who made me what I am: a capable woman... and a loving mom.

For now, and maybe forever, that's enough.

AND FINALLY...

Now that I've shared some of the heartbreaking, wonderful, stressful, funny, lonely, and joyful aspects of being a single parent, I hope you've learned a smidgen from my mistakes, or at least had a good belly laugh at my foibles.

At the very least I hope you now believe that the term "single parenthood" is NOT an oxymoron. It IS possible to be a successful single parent, with lots of prayer, of course. Whenever I hear someone say my children came from a "broken" home, I bristle and remind them that my home was "broken" BEFORE my divorce, and I FIXED it! I will always believe that raising children in a happy single-parent family is infinitely better than bringing them up midst the pain, abuse, and anguish that a truly broken marriage often reaps.

I'd like to leave you with three suggestions. The first is to learn to laugh at yourself and your mistakes. Don't take yourself or your children too seriously. Lighten up, have fun. Enjoy each other. Make up fish tales around the dinner table. Get silly. Laughter is the best stress reducer there is.

Second, be open to change. As your children grow up and leave home, one by one, you must create new adventures and new friends for yourself. It takes effort to make new friends. Do it. Luckily, these days there are plenty of ways to meet interesting people of all ages. And don't forget that in order to have friends, you must be a friend. So pick up the phone and get something organized.

Also, whether you're a new single parent or one who's been doing the job for years, you'll never know when someone new will walk into your life. Someone who makes you hear bells and whistles when the room is silent. Someone who becomes a soul mate and who will cherish you and your children hand in hand, heart to heart, for the rest of your lives.

If God brings someone truly special into your life, don't be afraid to make another commitment. Just don't rush it. Psychologists say it takes three to five years to get over a divorce or death of a spouse. You need those years to grieve, heal, and become whole again. Only then are you truly ready to enter into another relationship.

And finally, make God the head of your household. We all know that single parenting is a challenge of monumental proportions. You may have days when you're so stressed or unhappy you wonder if you can go on. Believe me: you can. Join a church, get involved, ask for help when you need it, volunteer to help others whenever you can. Just remember, with God at the helm of your family, there's no end to what you can accomplish.

God bless you and your children. You *are* a family.